Josiah Royce

THE SOURCES OF
RELIGIOUS INSIGHT

with a new introduction and index by
Frank M. Oppenheim, S.J.

The Catholic University of America Press

Washington, D.C.

First published in 1912
Introduction and index copyright © 2001
The Catholic University of America Press
All rights reserved
Printed in the United States of America

Library of Congress Cataloging-in-Publication Data

Royce, Josiah, 1855–1916.
   The sources of religious insight / Josiah Royce ; with a new
introduction and index by Frank M. Oppenheim.
       p   cm.
Originally published: New York : C. Scribner's Sons, 1912.
Includes bibliographical references and index.
ISBN 0-8132-1073-9 (pbk. : alk. paper)
1. Religion-Philosophy.   I. Title.
BL51 .R6   2001
210-dc21   00-047356

SUMMARY OF CONTENTS

II

INDIVIDUAL EXPERIENCE AND SOCIAL EXPERIENCE AS SOURCES OF RELIGIOUS INSIGHT

III

THE OFFICE OF THE REASON

IV

THE WORLD AND THE WILL

V

THE RELIGION OF LOYALTY

VI

THE RELIGIOUS MISSION OF SORROW

I. The consideration of Loyalty leads over to a new problem. "Tribulation" as a hindrance to religious insight. Reasons why this is the case, introduced by a statement regarding our experience of evil. The principle that "Evil ought to be altogether put out of existence" stated, and

VII

THE UNITY OF THE SPIRIT AND THE INVISIBLE CHURCH

INTRODUCTION

In November 1911, at Lake Forest, Illinois, Josiah Royce delivered his Bross Lectures, soon published as *The Sources of Religious Insight*. Of this work Royce wrote, "It is one of the easiest of my books to read, —so I fancy. And it contains the whole sense of me in a brief compass."[1]

When R. B. Perry drafted a famous biographical sketch of Royce, J. Loewenberg, Royce's most trusted assistant, cautioned him not to omit the *Sources*. For Royce had described it as his *Sonnenklarer Bericht*.[2] Significantly, John Clendenning, a leading Royce scholar, dedicated four pages to the *Sources* in his recently revised *Life* of Royce.

Despite these and other appraisals,[3] rarely has a treasure been more overlooked. Yet this overlooking of the *Sources* can readily be understood. An easy read, it hides its depths and can easily be mistaken as less than genuine philosophy. Its enticing sim-

1. *Letters of Josiah Royce,* ed. John Clendenning (Chicago: University of Chicago Press, 1970), 570.

2. Royce's *Sources* was "an account brighter than the sun," *sic* J. Loewenberg to R. B. Perry, 18 August, 1929; Perry Papers, Harvard Archives.

3. Moreover, John E. Smith of Yale regards the *Sources* as "very important"; Vincent Potter, S.J., of Fordham treasured it highly; and I recorded my appreciation of it in my *Royce's Mature Philosophy of Religion* (Notre Dame, Ind.: University of Notre Dame Press, 1987), chaps. 6–8.

plicity masks how profoundly and compactly Royce wrote many of its lines. Even a person only minimally acquainted with the broad sweep of Royce's writings may find it hard to believe that this work contains within its brief compass the "whole sense" of Royce. Yet he witnessed just that to Deakin, his long-time Australian friend.

Then too, Royce's late masterpiece, *The Problem of Christianity,* was published only one year after the *Sources.* This distracted attention from the *Sources.* Empowered by Royce's own originality and his late profound insight into Peirce's thought, the *Problem* rightly calls for more study than the *Sources.* In sum, these are a few factors that have led many to bypass the *Sources*—something Royce cautioned against in his Preface to *The Problem of Christianity.*

Little wonder, then, that in effect the *Sources* fell "stillborn from the press." On the eve of World War I many educated Americans failed to recognize two facts about the *Sources.* It carefully refined the deepest and most intimate religious experience of human beings, and it provided an urgently needed counterbalance to William James's *Varieties of Religious Experience.*

In the *Sources* Royce intended neither to sketch a general philosophy of religion nor to focus on a philosophy of the Christian religion.[4] Rather, he wanted to focus more sharply on some "springs" in

4. This latter endeavor would occupy him a year later in the *Problem.*

human consciousness from which, if integrated, authentic religious insight arises. Instead of investigating the whole of religious experience, Royce chose to focus on such religious knowledge as is found experientially in the saving presence (or indirectly, in the absence) of that Reality to which Royce referred as the Deliverer (or Deliverance). He found this experiential knowledge mediated basically through a combination of individual and social experience. Then these were serially enriched by reason, will, and dedicated loyalty. In this way these synthesized sources reached initial authenticity. However, the insightful religious knowledge found in genuine loyalty needed to be purified further by undergoing the illumining mission of atoning sorrow and then the enlightenment of life lived in the unity of the Spirit.

Royce did not intend that his cumulation of seven sources should form an exhaustive listing of the inner fonts of religious insight. Both he and friends commenting on his text pointed out other "sources of religious insight." These included the world of nature itself, along with beauty, prayer, and the sense of fulfillment at a task well done. To this list were added right ethical decision-making, the pragmatic test of practical religious living, mystical experiences, the cult of the dead, and finally "revelation" (whether spelled with a small or a large "r"). As a matter of fact, Royce was quite aware of the limited scope of his own endeavor.

As mentioned, his style in the *Sources* is simple—almost too simple, since it hides the surprising contents and the deep investigative procedure which its current carries along. After his upbringing in an evangelical tradition, Royce chose to belong to no visible Christian tradition. Yet unlike many philosophers, he held that many truths, urgently needed for salvation, lay hidden within the biblical tradition. These truths made up for him what he called the two-edged "sword of the spirit."

For instance, if human selves are united with the Spirit, they are on the path of salvation. Yet if they are alienated (or "detached") from a genuine community and its Spirit, theirs is the "moral burden of the detached individual," in need of reunion with the Spirit. Moreover, atoning grace has a role to play if individuals, detached from a saving group, are to be led back to the homeland of a Beloved Community.

Royce realized that this vital core of the biblical tradition needed to be purified. For historically it had become encrusted with certain legends, myths, and various cultural elements distinctive of the Near East, Greece, and Rome. Yet he never doubted the power of the Bible's vital core to engender a higher life in human selves and lead them to meaningful lives.

In fact, his philosophical reflection on biblical ideas, while irritating some secularists, distinguishes Royce from the other classical American philosophers. A person can scarcely scan any two pages of his non-logical writings without encountering a quotation, allusion, image, or phrase from the Bible. Thus Royce stands out, much like Jonathan Edwards of old, as a clear voice to all Americans whose lives are based on the Bible.

Besides his simple but compact and profound style in the *Sources* and his biblical flavor, what *distinctive themes* can the reader expect to find here? In this Introduction, I invite the reader, who may here discover other key ideas, to notice in the *Sources* seven major themes: the religious paradox, insight, religious insight, sorrow's religious mission, Royce's reflective method, his symbolism of light, and genuine loyalty.

1. In the *Sources*, Royce studies one aspect of religious experience in general. His study pivots upon the *"religious paradox,"* or what Royce at times calls the "paradox of revelation."[5] Parallel paradoxes are found in common sense and science (105), but in the *Sources* the paradox lies in some process of revelation. For whatever external revelation(s) may intervene in an individual's life, "something inside" must render one operationally sure that he or she "already knows the essential marks by which a divine revelation is to be distinguished from any other sort of report" (23).

What sort of "interior light" or "insight" might this be? It must acquaint one so personally with the

5. *Sources,* 20–25. In the text, references within parentheses are to the *Sources.*

divine nature that, when one experiences what seems a divine "message," one securely discerns (or recognizes) the divine handwriting and signature. Or, as Royce put it succinctly, "without the witness of the spirit in the heart, no external revelation could enlighten those who are in darkness" (24).

Each human self, then, requires that "interior light" whereby he sees that he (a) needs divine deliverance; (b) sees the right way to it; and (c) also sees "what the divine nature and expression essentially involves" (24).

Accordingly, Royce's task in the *Sources* lies in scrutinizing consciousness in search of those various "inner beams" which must converge before an authentic non-deceptive light (or insight) can dawn reliably. Hence, his central question becomes, "What are these conscious religious 'beams' and how tell when they are so self-reinstating as to be genuine?"

Of course, John Dewey's critique against "questing for certitude" aptly applies to most other matters. But when it comes to discerning safely one's path to religious salvation or otherwise ending up being duped into ultimate foolishness, one meets a uniquely different matter. For at this deepest level of personal spiritual identity, one is rightly concerned about the precariousness of human life, seeing here that one can waste one's life utterly.

2. "Insight" is a term that marks the Royce of his late middle period (1908–11). Insight blooms in con-

sciousness after many empirical facts have been accumulated, their relationships understood, their wider connections to the universe reasoned about, and then all of these mused over until there occurs a breakthrough to a new, intimate level knowledge. For Royce, insight at least synthesizes descriptive and appreciative knowledges. As he put it:

Insight is knowledge that makes us aware of the unity of many facts in one whole, and that at the same time brings us into intimate personal contact with these facts and with the whole wherein they are united. The three marks of insight are breadth of range, coherence and unity of view, and closeness of personal touch. (5–6)

3. Furthermore, such insight becomes religious when its objects are characteristically religious. As interpretive and almost intuitive knowledge, *religious insight* comprises not only a grasp of one's most important goal (or ideal) and one's great danger of missing this goal because of one's own inadequate resources, but also some encounter with the Deliverer. The human self experiences this Deliverance as:

. . . the presence or the coming or the longing for, or the communion with something which he comes to view as the power that may save him from his need, or as the light that may dispel his darkness, or as the truth that shows him the way out, or as the great companion who helps him—in a word, as his Deliverer. (28–29)

Here Royce's flexibility about various ways to experience the Deliverer (even in "his" absence by being felt in one's longing for "him") and about various ways of interpreting this "presence" deserves notice by those who tend to charge Royce with "fixed" modes and content of thought.

The fruit, then, of this religious insight is knowledge of the need and the way of salvation. Human wisdom can name no more basically important kind of knowledge.

4. Royce's highlighting of the *"religious mission of sorrow"* supplies another distinctive theme of the *Sources.* The problem of evil touched Royce very personally—in a challenging marital relation, in his straightened financial circumstances, in the late rejection of his doctrines by many philosophers, and especially in the deaths, a short time previously, of his gifted son, Christopher, and of his closest friend, William James. Little wonder, then, that Royce's decades-long musings on the problem of evil constitute both the neuralgic point of his philosophy and its engendering seed.

This led him to two accomplishments. He wrote more on the problem of evil than did any other classical American philosopher. And he taught that by an idealizing process one can creatively transform sufferings into "sorrows" that reveal new possibilities and wider ranges of perspective. Doing so sends (or missions) one to that higher knowledge wherein one glimpses a previously unrecognized realm of spiritual truth and unity. And this glimpse empowers one to loyal and perhaps even atoning service.

Royce's distinctive doctrine about sorrow's religious mission rests on the hard truth that when one transforms suffering into sorrow, one can catch a glimpse of one's genuine homeland of the spirit and the way to it.

5. Royce's *reflective method* undergirds his way of validating the seven sources of religious insight. He developed this method upon the basis of Socrates's famous method of cross-questioning students with care. Royce's reflective method consists in the experience of encountering both a performative contradiction and the light it creates.

For instance, try to *deny* that you need to be involved individually if you are to envision your religious ideal, sense your need for it, and endeavor to embody it personally. Attempting this denial, you experience, as an absolute operational requirement, that to truly know these three religious objects, you must be involved individually. In this way Royce finds in the individual the rock from which springs his first source of religious insight.

Or again, turning to his second or social source of religious insight, try to deny that you need the help of others. Your very denial cannot be uttered unless it is directed to someone. Hence, your attempt at total individualism involves you in a performative contradiction. For with your lips you utter what in your heart you know to be absolutely false since it contradicts your lived operation.

Royce continues this reflective method throughout the remaining five sources of religious insight. He thus generates the seven operational or experientially discovered absolutes that secure his procedure in this work and validate the genuineness of the sources he discovers.[6]

6. By his choice of the term "insight," Royce committed himself to the *symbolism of both light and the sight which light enables.* On the positive side, this united Royce with a symbol common to, and embedded in, all religions round the world—both of the primitive and of the more refined kinds. It thus contributed to his ecumenical intent. On the problematic side, this choice of the symbolism of light involved him in what is sometimes called the enigma of the "little hidden foxes." That is, little foxes have ways of inserting themselves undetected in certain hen houses. Similarly, "beams of light" can arise in human consciousness from what seem to be natural sources *alone.* Yet perhaps simultaneously the "little fox" of a divine spirit is also inserting itself undetected to prompt these intimate "beams" or insights.

This enigma of the little hidden foxes often occasions a futile battle about the roles of the "natural" and the "supernatural" in human religious life. It can also entrap and mislead the incautious reader of the *Sources* who fails to recognize that Royce employs "natural" and "supernatural," "human" and "superhuman," in his own *unique* way.

6. For instance, see *Sources,* 266–72.

For Royce, *direct* experience of facts and relations that lie beyond our human span of consciousness lies beyond our nature. Accordingly, these are "supernatural," "superhuman," and "superindividual." Yet, according to his principle of idealism, such facts and relations cannot be real unless some direct experiencing of them is occurring. This implies, however, the reality of forms of consciousness that are "superhuman" in the sense of higher-than-*individually*-human consciousness. These superindividual forms of consciousness are *"living, intelligent, organic unities,"*[7] communities or "minded beings" which enjoy "the unity of the spirit." By this term Royce "name[d] simply the *unity of meaning which belongs to these superhuman forms of consciousness"* (271).

7. Finally, in pointing to *genuine loyalty* as a source of religious insight, Royce does not tire of pointing out that the Cause is not an abstraction or some ethereal ideal, but rather a concrete, real, spiritual unity (199–200). As he said elsewhere, for the loyal the Cause is a concrete living Community, a personal intelligent "minded being" with its own life and will. It is as concrete a reality as is a family of father, mother, and their child.

To such a reality the genuinely loyal self dedicates itself. By doing so, he or she is opened up to

7. With this phrase John E. Smith renders Royce's idea of a community or his "second level" of reality; see p. 36 of his Introduction to the 1968 Chicago edition of the *Problem,* reprinted in the Catholic University of America Press edition, 2001.

the Great Community of all human selves, and even to the Universal Community of all "minded beings." This opening up and higher orientation derive from the mediation of the Beloved Community of atonement, whose members are its graced and atoning "genuine loyalists."

In the end, then, the reader is left with the enigma whether the profundity of vision of the *Sources* or its simplicity of style is the more artful.

Frank Oppenheim, S.J.
Xavier University
Cincinnati, Ohio
January 1, 2001

I

THE RELIGIOUS PROBLEM AND THE HUMAN INDIVIDUAL

I

THE RELIGIOUS PROBLEM AND THE HUMAN INDIVIDUAL

My first task must be to forestall possible disappointments regarding the scope of our inquiry. In seven lectures upon a vast topic very little can at best be accomplished. I want to tell you at the outset what are some of the limitations to which I propose to subject my undertakings.

I come before you as a philosophical inquirer addressing a general audience of thoughtful people. This definition of my office implies from the outset very notable limitations. As a philosophical inquirer I am not here to preach to you, but to appeal to your own thoughtfulness. Again, since my inquiry concerns the Sources of Religious Insight, you will understand, I hope, that I shall not undertake to present to you any extended system of religious doctrine. Upon sources of insight we are to concentrate our attention. What insight may be obtained from those sources we shall only attempt to indicate in the most general way, not at length to expound. What theologians would call a system of dogmas, I shall not undertake to define. What philosophers would regard as a comprehensive philosophy of religion I shall have no time to develop within our limits. I am to make some comments upon the ways in which religious truths can become accessible to men. What truths thus become accessible you must in large measure discover by your own appeal to the sources of which I shall try to tell you.

These somewhat narrow limitations may have, as I hope, their correlative advantages. Since I am to speak of sources, rather than of creeds or of philosophies, I may be able to appeal to people of decidedly various opinions without directing undue attention to the motives that divide them. I need not presuppose that my hearers are of the company of believers or of the company of doubters; and if they are believers, it matters little, for my present purpose, to what household of the faith they belong. I am not here to set people right as to matters of doctrine, but rather to point out the way that, if patiently followed, may tend to lead us all toward light and unity of doctrine. If you listen to my later lectures you may, indeed, be led to ask various questions about my own creed, which, in these lectures, I shall not attempt to answer. But I shall be content if what I say helps any of you, however little, toward finding for yourselves answers to your own religious questions.

I

The limitations of my task, thus indicated, will become still clearer if I next try to define the term Religious Insight as I intend it to be here understood.

And first I must speak briefly of the word Insight. By insight, whatever the object of insight may be, one means some kind of knowledge. But the word insight has a certain richness of significance whereby we distinguish what we call insight from knowledge in general. A man knows the way to the office where he does his business. But if he is a successful man, he has insight into the nature and rules of his business and into the means whereby success is attained. A man knows the names and the faces of his acquaintances. But he has some sort of insight into the characters of his familiar friends. As these examples suggest, insight is a name for a special sort and degree of knowledge. Insight is knowledge that unites a certain breadth of range, a certain wealth of acquaintance together with a certain unity and coherence of grasp, and with a certain closeness of intimacy whereby the one who has insight is brought into near touch with the objects of his insight. To repeat: Insight is knowledge that makes us aware of the unity of many facts in one whole, and that at the same time brings us into intimate personal contact with these facts and with the whole wherein they are united. The three marks of insight are breadth of range, coherence and unity of view, and closeness of personal touch. A man may get some sort of *sight* of as many things as you please. But if we have insight, we view some connected whole of things, be this whole a landscape as an artist sees it, or as a wanderer surveys it from a mountain top, or be this whole an organic process as a student of the sciences of life aims to comprehend it, or a human character as an appreciative biographer tries to portray it. Again, we have insight when, as I insist, our acquaintance with our object is not only coherent but close and personal. Insight you cannot obtain at second hand. You can learn by rote and by hearsay many things; but if you have won insight, you have won it not without the aid of your own individual experience. Yet experience is not by itself sufficient to produce insight unless the coherence and the breadth of range which I have just mentioned be added.

Insight may belong to the most various sorts of people and may be concerned with the most diverse kinds of objects. Many very unlearned people have won a great deal of insight into the matters that intimately concern them. Many very learned people. have attained almost no insight into anything. Insight is no peculiar possession of the students of any technical specialty or of any one calling. Men of science aim to reach insight into the objects of their researches; men of affairs, or men of practical efficiency, however plain or humble their calling, may show insight of a very high type, whenever they possess knowledge that bears the marks indicated, knowledge that is intimate and personal and that involves a wide survey of the unity of many things.

Such, then, is insight in general. But I am to speak of Religious Insight. Religious insight must be distinguished from other sorts of insight by its object, or by its various characteristic objects. Now, I have no time to undertake, in this opening discourse, any adequate definition of the term Religion or of the features that make an object a religious object. Religion has a long and complex history, and a tragic variety of forms and of objects of belief. And so religion varies prodigiously in its characteristics from age to age, from one portion of the human race to another, from one individual to another. If we permitted ourselves to define religion so as merely to insist upon what is common to all its forms, civilised and savage, our definition would tend to become so inclusive and so attenuated as to be almost useless for the purposes of the present brief inquiry. If, on the other hand, we defined religion so as to make the term denote merely what the believer in this or in that creed thinks of as his own religion, we should from the start cut ourselves off from the very breadth of view which I myself suppose to be essential to the highest sort of re-

ligious insight. Nobody fully comprehends what
religion is who imagines that his own religion is the
only genuine religion. As a fact, I shall therefore
abandon at present the effort to give a technically
finished definition of what constitutes religion, or
of the nature of the religious objects. I shall here
limit myself to a practically useful preliminary
mention of a certain feature that, for my present
purpose, shall be viewed as the essential characteristic of religion, and of religious objects, so far as
these lectures propose to discuss religion.

The higher religions of mankind—religions such
as Buddhism and Christianity—have had in common this notable feature, namely, that they have
been concerned with the problem of the Salvation
of Man. This is sometimes expressed by saying
that they are redemptive religions—religions interested in freeing mankind from some vast and universal burden, of imperfection, of unreasonableness,
of evil, of misery, of fate, of unworthiness, or of sin.
Now, for my present purposes, this *interest in the
salvation of man* shall be made, in these lectures, the
essential feature of religion in so far as religion shall
here be dealt with. The religious objects, whatever
they otherwise may prove to be, shall be defined as
objects such that, when we know them, and in case
we can know them, this knowledge of them helps
to show us the way of salvation. The central and
essential postulate of whatever religion we, in these
lectures, are to consider, is *the postulate that man*

needs to be saved. And religious insight shall for us mean insight into the way of salvation and into those objects whereof the knowledge conduces to salvation.

This preliminary definition, thus somewhat abruptly stated, will arouse in the minds of many of you serious doubts and questions. And only the whole course of our study can serve to furnish such answer to these doubts and questions as I can hope to supply to you. Yet a further word or two of purely preliminary explanation may help to prevent your thoughts, at this point, from being turned in a wrong direction. I have defined religious insight as insight into the way of salvation. But what, you may ask, do I mean by the salvation of man or by man's need of salvation? To this question I still owe you a brief preliminary answer.

II

The word salvation naturally first suggests to your own mind certain familiar traditions which have played a great part in the history of Christianity. I do not mean to make light of those traditions nor yet of the significance of the historical Christianity to which they belong. Yet, as I have already told you, these lectures will have no dogmatic religious system to expound, and, for that very reason, will not attempt the grave task of any extended discussion of Christianity. I propose at some future time, not in these lectures, but upon a wholly different occasion, to attempt an application of some of the principles that underlie the present lectures to the special problems which Christianity offers to the student of religion. But these lectures are not to be directly concerned with this special task of expounding or interpreting or estimating Christian doctrines. I repeat: My limited undertaking is to consider in company with you the sources of religious insight, not the contents of any one religion. You will understand, therefore, that when I define religious insight as insight into the way of salvation, I use the word salvation in a sense that I wish you to conceive in terms much more general than those which certain Christian traditions have made familiar to you.

I have already said that both Buddhism and Christianity are interested in the problem of the salvation of mankind, and share in common the postulate that man needs saving. I could have named still other of the world's higher religions which are characterised by the same great interest. Had I the time and the technical knowledge, I could show you how far backward in time, how deep down into the very essence of some of the religions that seem to us extremely primitive, this concern for man's salvation, and for a knowledge of the way of salvation, extends. But the history of religion does not fall within my present scope. And to the varieties of religious doctrine I can only allude by

way of illustration.   Yet the mere mention of such
varieties may serve, I hope, to show you that whole
nations and races, and that countless millions of
men, have conceived of their need for salvation,
and have sought the way thereto, while they have
known nothing of Christian doctrine, and while they
have not in the least been influenced by those dogmas regarding the fall of man, the process of re-
demption, or the future destiny of the soul of man
which are brought to your minds when you hear
the word salvation.

Be willing, then, to generalise our term and to
dissociate the idea of salvation from some of the
settings in which you usually have conceived it.
Since there is thus far in our discussion no question
as to whose view of the way of salvation is the true
view, you can only gain by such a dissociation, even
if it be but a temporary effort at generalisation.
The cry of humanity for salvation is not a matter
of any one time or faith.   The pathos of that cry
will become only the deeper when you learn to see
why it is so universal a cry.   The truth, if there be
any accessible truth, regarding the genuine way of
salvation will become only the more precious to
you when you know by how widely sundered paths
the wanderers in the darkness of this world have
sought for the saving light.

So let me next attempt to define salvation in
a sufficiently general sense.   Man is an infinitely
needy creature.   He wants endlessly numerous spe-

cial things—food, sleep, pleasure, fellowship, power
in all its Protean shapes, peace in all its elusive
forms, love in its countless disguises—in brief, all
the objects of desire. But amongst these infinitely
manifold needs, the need for salvation stands out,
in the minds of those who feel it, as a need that is
peculiarly paramount, so that, according to their
view of life, to desire salvation is to long for some
pearl of great price, for the sake of which one
would be ready to sell all that one has. The idea
that man needs salvation depends, in fact, upon two
simpler ideas whereof the main idea is constituted.
*The first is the idea that there is some end or aim of
human life which is more important than all other
aims, so that, by comparison with this aim all else is
secondary and subsidiary, and perhaps relatively unim-
portant, or even vain and empty. The other idea is
this: That man as he now is, or as he naturally is, is
in great danger of so missing this highest aim as to
render his whole life a senseless failure by virtue of
thus coming short of his true goal.* Whoever has been
led to conceive human life in these terms, namely, to
think that there is for man some sort of highest
good, by contrast with which all other goods are
relatively trivial, and that man, as he is, is in great
danger of losing this highest good, so that his greatest need is of escape from this danger—whoever, I
say, thus views our life, holds that man needs salvation.

Now, I beg you to observe that such a view of

life as this is in no wise dependent upon any one dogma as to a future state of reward and punishment, as to heaven and hell, as to the fall of man, or as to any point of the traditional doctrine of this or of that special religion.   Philosophers and prophets, and even cynics, learned and unlearned men, saints and sinners, sages and fanatics, Christians and non-Christians, believers in immortality and believers that death ends all, may agree, yes, have agreed, in viewing human life in the general spirit just characterised.   A very few examples may serve to show how wide-spread this longing for salvation has been and how manifold have also been its guises.

I have already mentioned Buddhism as a religion that seeks the salvation of man.   The central idea of the original southern Buddhism, as you know, is pessimistic.   Man, so the Buddha and his earlier followers taught, is naturally doomed to misery. This doom is so pervasive and so fatal that you in vain would seek to escape from it through any luxuries, or, so to speak, excesses, of good fortune. On the throne or in the dungeon, wealthy or a beggar, man is always (so the Buddhist insists) the prisoner of desire, a creature of longing, consumed by the fires of passion—and therefore miserable. For man's will is insatiable, and hence always disappointed.   Now we are here not in the least concerned with estimating this pessimism.   This gloomy ancient Indian view of existence may be as false as you please. Enough—millions of men have held it, and therefore have longed for salvation. For if, as the early Buddhists held, the evil of human life is thus pervasive and paramount, then the aim of escaping from such fatal ill must be deeper and more important than any economic aim or than any intent to satisfy this or that special desire. If man is naturally doomed to misery, the escape from this natural doom must be at once the hardest and the highest of human tasks. The older Buddhism undertakes to accomplish this task by teaching the way to "the extinction of desire" and by thus striking at "the root of all misery." In Nirvana, those who have attained the goal have won their way beyond all desire. They return not. They are free from the burden of human existence. Such is one view of the need and the way of salvation.

If we turn in a wholly different direction, we find Plato, in the great myth of the "Phædrus," in the arguments and myths of the "Republic," and in various other famous passages, defining what he regards as the true goal of the human soul, portraying how far we have naturally come short of that goal, and pointing out a way of salvation. And, in another age, Marcus Aurelius writes his "Thoughts" in the interest of defining the end for which it is worth while to live, the bondage and failure in which the foolish man actually lives, and the way out of our foolishness.

But are the partisans of ways of salvation confined to such serious and unworldly souls as were the early Buddhists and the ancient moralists? No; turn to modern times. Read the stanzas into which Fitzgerald, in a highly modern spirit, very freely translated the expressions of an old Persian poet—Omar Khayyam; or, again, read the great programme of Nietzsche's ethical and religious revolt as set forth only a few years since in his "Zarathustra"; or recall Goethe's "Faust"; remember even Byron's "Manfred"; and these few instances from amongst a vast wealth of more or less recent literary examples will show you that the idea of salvation and the search for salvation are matters that belong to no one type of piety or of poetry or of philosophy. Cynics and rebels, ancient sages and men who are in our foremost rank of time, can agree, and have agreed, in maintaining that there is some goal of life, conceivable, or at least capable of being, however dimly, appreciated—some goal that, if accessible, would fulfil and surpass our lesser desires, or would save us from our bondage to lesser ills, while this goal is something that we naturally miss, or that we are in great danger of missing—so that, whatever else we need, we need to be saved from this pervasive and overmastering danger of failure.

"Oh love, could thou and I with fate conspire
To grasp this sorry scheme of things entire,
    Would we not shatter it to bits and then,
Remould it nearer to the heart's desire?"

Thus Fitzgerald's Omar expresses, in rebellious speech, the need of salvation. "What is your greatest hour?"—so begins Nietzsche's Zarathustra in his opening address to the people. And he replies: "It is the hour of your great contempt"— the hour, so he goes on to explain, when you despise all the conventional values and trivial maxims of a morality and a religion that have become for you merely traditional, conventional, respectable, but infinitely petty. Now, if you observe that St. Paul's epistle to the Romans, despite its utterly different religious ideas, begins with an analogous condemnation of the social world as it was, or as it always naturally is, you may learn to appreciate the universal forms in which the need for salvation comes to men's consciousness, however various their creed. Swinburne's well-known chorus sums up man's life as it is, thus:

> "He weaves and is clothed with derision,
>   Sows, and he shall not reap;
> His life is a watch or a vision
>   Between a sleep and a sleep."

Such, then, is man's need. "Here we have no continuing city, we seek a city out of sight"—such is another expression of this same need. What I ask you to do, just here, is to catch a glimpse of this universal form of the need for salvation. As you see, there is always a certain element of gloom and tragedy involved in the first conception of this need.

All depends, for the further fortunes of one's religious consciousness, upon whether or not one can get insight into the true nature of this need and into the way toward the needed salvation.

III

Religious Insight means then, for my present purposes, *insight into the need and into the way of salvation.* If the problem of human salvation has never come home to your mind, as a genuine problem of life and of experience, you will feel no interest in religion in the sense to which the present lectures will arbitrarily confine the term. If, on the other hand, your live personal experience has made you intimate with any form or phase of this problem of the pathetic need and cry of man for salvation, then I care not, at least at the outset of these discourses, whether you have thought of this problem in theological or in secular, in reverent or in rebellious, or in cynical terms, whether you have tried to solve it by scientific or by sentimental or by traditional means, or whether the problem now takes shape in your mind as a problem to be dealt with in a spirit of revolt or of conformity, of sceptical criticism or of intuitive faith, of hope or of despair. What we want is insight, if insight be possible, into the way of salvation. The problem with which these lectures are to deal is: What are the sources of such insight?

At the outset of our effort to deal with this problem, I shall try to show how the experience of the individual human being is related to the issues that are before us. That is, in this and in part of our next lecture, I shall discuss the sense in which the individual experience of any one of us is a source of insight into the need and the way of salvation. Hereby we shall erelong be led to our social experience as a source of still richer religious insight. And from these beginnings we shall go on to a study of sources which are at once developments from these first mentioned sources, and sources that are much more significant than these first ones would be if they could be isolated from such developments. I ask you to follow my discourse in the same spirit of tolerance for various opinions and with the same effort to understand the great common features and origins of the religious consciousness—with the same spirit and effort, I say, by which I have tried to be guided in what I have already said to you in this introduction. It is always easy to see that, in religion, one man thinks thus and another man thinks otherwise, and that no man knows as much as we all wish to know. But I want to lay stress upon those perennial sources from which human insight has flowed and for ages in the future will continue to flow. To understand what these sources are will help us, I believe, toward unity of spirit, toward co-operation in the midst of all our varieties of faith, and toward insight itself and the fruits of insight.

IV

I can best undertake my brief initial study of the way in which the experience of the individual human being is a source of religious insight by meeting an objection that a reading of my printed programme may have aroused in the minds of some of you. My list of the sources of religious insight, as contained in the titles of these lectures, makes no express reference to a source which some of you will be disposed to regard as the principal source, namely, Revelation. Here, some of you will already have said, is a very grave omission. Man's principal insight into the need and the way of salvation comes, and must come, you will say, from without, from the revelation that the divine power which saves, makes of itself, through Scripture or through the Church. Now, so far as this thesis forms part of the doctrine of a particular religion, namely, in your own case, of Christianity, I shall in these lectures omit any direct discussion of that thesis. The reason for the omission I have already pointed out. These lectures undertake a limited task, and must be judged by their chosen limitations. But in so far as revelation is a general term, meaning whatever intercourse there may be between the divine and the human, all these lectures, in dealing with sources of religious insight, will be dealing with processes of revelation. And in what sense this assertion is true we shall see as we go on with our undertaking. This first mention of revelation enables me, however, both to state and to answer the objection to my programme which I have just mentioned, and in doing so to vindicate for the experience of any religiously disposed individual its true significance as a source of insight. Hereby, as I hope, I can forthwith show that even the present deliberately limited undertaking of these lectures has an importance which you ought to recognise, whatever your own views about revelation may be.

Let me suppose, then, that an objector, speaking on behalf of revelation as the main source of religious insight, states his case briefly thus: "Man learns of his need for salvation chiefly through learning what God's will is, and through a consequent discovery that his own natural will is not in conformity with God's will. He learns about the way of salvation by finding out by what process God is willing to save him. Both sorts of knowledge must be principally mediated through God's revelation of himself, of his will, and of his plan of salvation. For, left to himself, man cannot find out these things. Apart from revelation, they are divine secrets. Hence the principal source of religious insight must be revelation."

Whoever states his case thus brings to our attention at this point what I may venture to name: The Religious Paradox, or, to use other terms, The Paradox of Revelation. I call attention to this paradox in no spirit of mere cavilling or quibbling. The importance of the matter the whole course of these lectures will show. The religious paradox, as we shall define it, is one of the deepest facts in all religious history and experience. It will meet us everywhere; and every devout soul daily faces it. Moreover, as we shall see, it is a special case of a paradox regarding our human insight which is as universal and pervasive, in its significance for us, as is our human intelligence itself. I call it here the religious paradox. I shall later show you that it might be called, just as correctly, the paradox of common-sense, the paradox of reason, the paradox of knowledge, yes, the paradox of being thoughtfully alive in any sense whatever.

The religious paradox, viewed as it first comes to us, may be stated thus: Let a man say: "I have this or this religious insight because God has revealed to me, thus and thus, his will about me and his plans; has taught me my need of salvation and the divine way of salvation.

> "'Man is blind because of sin;
>   Revelation makes him sure;
>   Without that who looks within,
>   Looks in vain; for all's obscure.'"

Let a man say this. At once, addressing this believer in a revelation, we must ask, in no jesting spirit, but with the fullest sense of the tragic gravity of the issue: "By what marks do you personally

distinguish a divine revelation from any other sort
of report?"

Consider for an instant what this question implies. A depositor at a bank, in signing a cheque,
reveals to his bank his will that such and such
funds, which he already has on deposit at the bank,
shall be paid to the order of a certain person. How
is the bank able to recognise this revelation of the
depositor's will? The answer is: The bank, acting
in the usual order of business, regards this revelation as genuine because its officers already know,
with sufficient assurance, the depositor's signature,
and can therefore recognise it at sight, subject, of
course, to a certain usually negligible risk of forgery.
Apply the principle here involved to the case of
the one who acknowledges the genuineness of a
divine revelation. In asserting: "I know that this
revelation is from God," the believer in the revelation asserts, in substance, that in some sense and
by some means he personally knows, as it were, the
divine signature; knows by what marks the divine
being reveals himself. This is the vast presumption, if you will, upon which the believer in revelation depends for his assurance. He knows God's
autograph. Now, how shall such a knowledge of
the divine autograph have arisen in the mind of the
individual believer? Has this believer first wandered through all the worlds to learn how the various orders of beings express themselves, what marks
of their wisdom and of their interest in humanity

they show, and who amongst them are, or who alone
is, actually divine?

I repeat—the stupendous question thus suggested
is one which I mention not in any spirit of cavil,
but solely for the sake of directing us on our further
way, and of calling attention at the outset to a fact
upon which all that is most vital in the religious
consciousness has in every age depended. Every
acceptance of a revelation, I say, depends upon
something that, in the individual's mind, must be
prior to this acceptance. And this something is an
assurance that the believer already knows the essential marks by which a divine revelation is to be
distinguished from any other sort of report. In
other words, a revelation can be viewed by you as
a divine revelation only in case you hold, for whatever reason, or for no reason, that you already are
acquainted with the signature which the divine will
attaches to its documents, that you know the marks
of any authentic revelation by which a divine will
can make itself known to you. Unless, then, you
are to make one supposed revelation depend for its
warrant upon another in an endless series, you must
presuppose that somewhere there is found a revelation that proves its genuineness by appealing to
what your own interior light, your personal acquaintance with the nature of a divine being, enables you
to know as the basis of all your further insight into
the divine. The one who appeals to revelation for
guidance cannot then escape from basing his appeal

upon something which involves a personal and individual experience of what the need and the way of salvation is and of what the divine nature and expression essentially involves.

Nor is this remark merely the unsympathetic comment of a philosophical critic of what passes for revelation. The truth of the remark is acknowledged by all those who have in one way or another insisted that, without the witness of the spirit in the heart, no external revelation could enlighten those who are in darkness; that miracles by themselves are inadequate, because signs and wonders cannot teach the divine will to those whom grace, working inwardly, does not prepare for enlightenment; and that, in brief, if there is any religious insight whatever accessible, it cannot come to us without our individual experience as its personal foundation.

Now, the religious paradox is this: What one pretends or at least hopes to know, when there is any question of religious insight, is something which has to do with the whole nature and destiny and duty and fate of man. For just such matters are in question when we talk, not of how to earn our living or of how to get this or that worldly prosperity, but about our need of salvation and about how to be saved. So deep and so weighty are these matters, that to pretend to know about them seems to involve knowing about the whole nature of things. And when we conceive of the whole nature

of things as somehow interested in us and in our salvation, as the religiously minded very generally do,
we call this nature of things divine, in a very familiar sense of that word.   Hence the higher religions generally undertake to know, as they say, the
divine.   And by the divine they mean some real
power or principle or being that saves us or that
may save us.   But how is this divine to be known?
By revelation?   But knowledge through revelation
can enlighten only the one in whose personal experience there is somewhere an adequate interior light,
which shines in the darkness, and which permits
him to test all revelations by a prior acquaintance
with the nature and marks and, so to speak, signature of the divine will.   Hereupon arises the question: How should I, weak of wit as I am, ignorant,
fallible, a creature of a day, come to possess that
intimate acquaintance with the plan of all things,
and with the meaning of life, and with the divine,
which I must obtain in case I am to pass upon the
marks whereby any revelation that can save me is
to be tested?   The paradox is that a being who is
so ignorant of his duty and of his destiny as to need
guidance at every point, so weak as to need saving,
should still hope, in his fallible experience, to get
into touch with anything divine.   The question is,
how is this possible?   What light can my individual
experience throw upon vast problems such as this?

V

I have stated what I call the religious paradox. The whole of what I have hereafter to tell you is needed in order to throw such light as I can here attempt to throw upon the solution of the paradox. You will not expect, then, an immediate answer to the question thus brought before you. Yet you see our present situation: Unless there is something in our individual experience which at least begins to bring us into a genuine touch, both with the fact that we need salvation and with the marks whereby we may recognise the way of salvation, and the essentially divine process, if such there be, which alone can save—unless, I say, there is within each of us something of this interior light by which saving divine truth is to be discerned, religious insight is impossible, and then no merely external revelation can help us. Let us then, without further delay, turn directly to the inner light, if such light there be, and ask what, apart from tradition, apart from external revelation, apart from explicit theories or reports concerning the universe, apart from all other sources, our own individual experience can tell us as to the need and the way of salvation, and as to the marks by which we may recognise whatever real influences, or divine beings, can intervene to help us in our need. We shall not upon this occasion answer the question; but we may do something to clarify the issue.

My dear friend, the late William James, in his book called "The Varieties of Religious Experience," defined, for his own purposes, religious experience as the experience of individuals who regard themselves as "alone with the divine." In portraying what he meant by "the divine," James emphasised, although in language different from what I am using, the very features about the objects of religious experience which I have just been trying to characterise in my own way. Those who have religious experience, according to James, get into touch with something which, as he says, gives "a new dimension" to their life. As a result of their better and more exalted religious experience, they win a sense of unity with "higher powers," whose presence seems to them to secure a needed but otherwise unattainable spiritual unity, peace, power in their lives. This "divine" thus accomplishes inwardly what the individual "alone with the divine" feels to be saving, to be needed, to be his pearl of great price. This is James's way of defining the objects of religious experience.

Now James's whole view of religious experience differs in many ways from mine. But just at the present point in our inquiry, where it is a question of what I should call the most elementary and intimate, but also the crudest and most capricious source of religious insight, namely, the experience of the individual "alone with the divine," I feel my own account to be most dependent upon that of

James and my own position to be most nearly in
agreement with his.

Let me refer you, then, at this stage, to James's
great collection and analysis of the facts of individual religious experience. Let me presuppose
some personal acquaintance, on your part, with
individual experiences of the various types that
James so wonderfully portrays. And then, in my
own way, and as independently of James's special
theories as possible, let me tell you what, to my
mind, is the essential substance of these elementary
religious experiences which may come to the individual when he is alone with the problem of his
own salvation and alone with his efforts to know
the divine that can save. Let me try to show you
that the individual, thus isolated, is indeed in touch
with a genuine source of insight. Let me try to
indicate both the value and the limitations of that
source in such wise as to prepare us to view this
first source in its needed relation to the sources
hereafter to be studied.

The religious experience of the individual may
concern three objects: First, his Ideal, that is, the
standard in terms of which he estimates the sense
and the value of his own personal life; secondly,
his Need of salvation, that is, the degree to which
he falls short of attaining his ideal and is sundered
from it by evil fortune, or by his own paralysis of
will, or by his inward baseness; thirdly, the presence or the coming or the longing for, or the com-

munion with something which he comes to view
as the power that may save him from his need, or
as the light that may dispel his darkness, or as the
truth that shows him the way out, or as the great
companion who helps him—in a word, as his Deliverer. The Ideal, the Need, the Deliverer—these
are the three objects which the individual experience, as a source of religious insight, has always
undertaken to reveal. James's collection of the
facts of religious experience richly illustrates what I
here have in mind. To that collection, and to your
own individual experience, I appeal as my warrant
for thus characterising our first source of insight.
Can we say that this source gives us genuine insight and is trustworthy? Does it teach us about
anything that is real; and if this be so, how far
does this source of insight go? What is the extent,
what are the limitations of the truth that one can
hope in this way to gain?

As to the first two objects of the individual religious experience, namely, the individual's own personal ideal and his sense of his need, you will
readily agree that one's private experience is, indeed,
a source of genuine insight. You will, however, find
it hard at first to define just how far that insight
extends. For the world of a man's private ideals
and estimates is a world of precious caprices, because not only does one man's private feelings or
intuitions about ideals and values differ from another
man's, but every man's own ideals, and his sense of

need, tend to alter endlessly with the play of his
passions, with the waxing and waning of all his
natural powers, with his health, with his age. One
form of the religious paradox may, in fact, be stated
thus: Without intense and intimate personal feeling, you never learn any valuable truths whatever
about life, about its ideals, or about its problems;
but, on the other hand, what you know only through
your feelings is, like the foam of the sea, unstable—
like the passing hour, doomed to pass away.

James, as a psychologist, well knew this truth
about the value and the limitations of private experience; yet it was characteristic of his enterprising
soul that he was always looking, in his "pluralistic
universe," for the strange, new religious experiences
of other and still other individuals, without being
able thereby even to define what all these ardent
souls were seeking, namely, some genuine home
land of the spirit, some place or experience or insight in which is to be revealed that for the sake of
which all the feelings, the caprices, the longings, the
efforts of individuals are justified—and fulfilled.

Now the best way of defining what it is which our
inner experience of our ideal and of our need shows
us is, I think, this: We are indeed, and so far
just as the Buddhists said, naturally the creatures
of transient feelings, of passing caprices, of various
and wilful longings. But, just because of this fact,
we can get an insight, as intimate as it is fragmentary, into one absolutely valuable ideal. I do not

think that the Buddhists best expressed our ideal
by the words "the extinction of desire." It is
rather the ideal of triumph over our unreason. It
is the ideal that the reign of caprice ought to be
ended, that the wounds of the spirit ought to be
healed. In the midst of all our (caprices,) yes,
because of our caprices, we learn the value of one
great spiritual ideal, the ideal of spiritual unity and
self-possession. And both our ideal and our need
come to consciousness at once. We need to bring
our caprices into some sort of harmony; to bind up
the wounds of what James calls the divided "self";
to change the wanderings of chance passion into
something that shall bring the home land of the
spirit, the united goal of life into sight. And so
much all the great cynics, and the nobler rebels,
and the prophets and the saints and the martyrs
and the sages have in common taught us. So
much Socrates and Plato and Marcus Aurelius, and
our modern teachers of the wisdom of life, and, in
his noblest words, the Buddha also, and Jesus,
have agreed in proclaiming as the ideal and the
need revealed to us by all that is deepest about our
individual experience: We need to give life sense,
to know and to control our own selves, to end the
natural chaos, to bring order and light into our
deeds, to make the warfare of natural passion subordinate to the peace and the power of the spirit.
This is our need. To live thus is our ideal. And
because this need is pressing and this ideal is far off
from the natural man, we need salvation.

[handwritten margin note:] sudden unexplained change in mood/behavior

So much, I say, our individual experience can bring before us. This ideal and this need can become the objects of an insight that is as intimate as it is, by itself, unsatisfying. This need, I think, all the devout share, however unlearned their speech, however simple their minds, however various their creeds. Unity of Spirit, conformity to an universal Will, peace with power—this is our need.

It remains for the individual experience to show to us, if it can, the presence of our Deliverer, the coming of that which we shall recognise as divine, just because it truly and authoritatively reveals to the Self the fulfilment that we need, by bringing us into touch with the real nature of things. We need to find the presence that can give this unity and self-possession to the soul. This presence is what all the higher religions seek to reveal. But if we are to learn of such an object of insight we must, indeed, come into touch with a Power or a Spirit that is in some true sense not-Ourselves. And so we must be able somehow to transcend the boundaries of any *merely* individual experience. Our individual experience must become some sort of intercourse with Another. And this Other must be in some sense the Master of Life, the Might that overcometh the world, the revealer of final truth. Without ceasing to be personal and intimate, our experience must in some way come into direct touch with the very nature of reality.

Is such a direct touch with the divine possible? The mystics of all ages have maintained that it is possible. Are they right? To answer this question adequately would be to solve the religious paradox. It would be to show whether and how the individual, even in his isolation, "alone with the divine," can come to be nevertheless in unity with all other spirits, in touch with all that lies beneath and above himself, and with all that constitutes the essence of reality. Perhaps this is indeed possible. Unless it is possible, revelation, as we have seen, loses precisely its most intimate significance, as an appeal of the divine spirit directly to the interior light. But, on the other hand, all the mystics confess that, *if* this is possible, and if it happens in their own cases, they alone, viewing their experience merely as an individual experience, know not *how* it happens, but must accept their revelation as an insight without knowing in what precise sense it is insight.

It follows that individual experience remains a source of religious insight as indispensable and as fundamental as it is, by itself, inadequate and in need of supplement. Unless you have inwardly felt the need of salvation, and have learned to hunger and thirst after spiritual unity and self-possession, all the rest of religious insight is to you a sealed book. And unless, in moments of peace, of illumination, of hope, of devotion, of inward vision, you have seemed to feel the presence of your Deliverer, unless it has sometimes *seemed* to you as if the way to the home land of the spirit were opened to your sight by a revelation as from the divine, unless this privilege has been yours, the way to a higher growth in insight will be slow and uncertain to you. But, on the other hand, no one who remains content with his merely individual experience of the presence of the divine and of his deliverer, has won the whole of any true insight. For, as a fact, we are all members one of another; and I can have no insight into the way of my salvation unless I thereby learn of the way of salvation for all my brethren. And there is no unity of the spirit unless all men are privileged to enter it whenever they see it and know it and love it.

Individual Experience, therefore, must abide with us to the very end of our quest, as one principal and fundamental source of insight. But it is one aspect only of Religious Experience. We shall learn to understand and to estimate it properly only when we have found its deeper relations with our Social Experience. In passing to our social experience, however, we shall not leave our individual experience behind. On the contrary, through thus passing to our social experience as a source of religious insight, we shall for the first time begin to see what our individual experience means.

II

INDIVIDUAL EXPERIENCE AND SOCIAL EXPERIENCE

II

INDIVIDUAL EXPERIENCE AND SOCIAL
EXPERIENCE

THE results of our first lecture appear to have
brought the religious problems, so far as we shall
attempt to consider them, into a position which in
one respect simplifies, in another respect greatly
complicates our undertaking.

I

In one way, I say, our undertaking is simplified.
For, as we have defined religion, the main concern
of any religion that we are to recognise is with the
salvation of man, and with whatever objects or
truths it is important to know if we are to find
the way of salvation. Now the experiences which
teach us that we need what I have ventured to call
by the traditional name salvation, are, from my
point of view, experiences common to a very large
portion of mankind. They are great and, in certain respects at least, simple experiences. You can
have them and estimate them without being committed to any one form of religious faith, without
accepting any special creed about supernatural

37

things, and even without hoping to find out any way of salvation whatever. The essential conditions for discovering that man needs salvation are these: You must find that human life has some highest end; and you must also find that man, as he naturally is, is in great danger of failing to attain this supreme goal. If you discover these two facts (and I personally hold them to be facts whose reality you can experience), then the quest for the salvation of man interests you, and is defined for you in genuinely empirical terms. Given the problem, you may or you may not see how to solve it. You may or you may not appeal to what you suppose to be a revelation to guide you on the way. But in any case, granted these conditions, granted that your experience has shown you your need of salvation—then the problem of religion is upon your hands. Soluble or insoluble, the topic of a revelation from above, or of a scientific inquiry, or of a philosophy, or of a haphazard series of efforts to better your condition, this problem, if it once comes to hold your attention, will make of you a religious inquirer. And so long as this is the case, no degree of cynicism or of despair regarding the finding of the way to salvation, will deprive you of genuinely religious interest. The issue will be one regarding facts of live experience. The concerns that for you will seem to be at stake will be perfectly human, and will be in close touch with every interest of daily life.

To conceive the business of religion in this way simplifies our undertaking, in so far as it connects religion not merely with doubtful dogmas and recondite speculations, but rather with personal and practical interests and with the spirit of all serious endeavour.

Upon the other hand, this way of defining religion does, indeed, also complicate certain aspects of our present task. For if, from our point of view, religion thus becomes, in one way or another, the concern of everybody who has once seen that life has a highest goal, and that we are all naturally in great danger of missing this goal—still any effort to study the nature of religious insight seems to require us to be somehow just to all the endless varieties of human opinion regarding what the highest goal of human life is, and regarding the way to attain that goal after we have once defined it. In some sense, in our further inquiry, nothing human can be alien to us, in case it involves any deep experience of man's purpose in living, or of man's peril as a seeker after the attainment of his purpose; or any assurance regarding the presence or the power which, entering into some sort of union with any man's own spiritual life, seems to that man an apt Deliverer from his evil plight, a genuinely saving principle in his life.

How great the resulting complications that threaten our investigation seem to be the conclusion of our former lecture showed us. Countless

souls, trusting to their individual experience, have
learned, as we at the last time indicated, to define
their ideal, and their need, and, upon occasion, to
discover the power that they took to be their saving
principle—their deliverer. Who amongst all these
were right, either in their judgment as to their
need or in their consciousness that they had found
the way that leads to peace, to triumph, to union
with the goal of human life? Were all of them
more or less right? Were any of them wholly
deluded? Are there as many supreme aims of life
as there are individuals? Are there as many ways
of salvation as there are religions that men follow?
And by what means shall we decide such questions?
Grave and infinitely complicated seem the issues
which these queries arouse.

Upon one side, then, our problem is pathetically
simple, human, practical, even commonplace. Daily
experience, in serious-minded people, illustrates it.
The plainest facts of our life exemplify it. It concerns nothing more recondite than that tragedy of
natural human failure which you may constantly
witness all about you, if not within you. Upon
the other side, no questions more bring you into
contact with the chaotic variety of human opinion,
and with the complexities of the whole universe,
than do the religious questions, when thus defined
in terms of men's deepest needs and of men's
hopes and faiths regarding the possible escape from
their most pressing peril of failure.

Our first lecture gave us a glimpse of this simplicity of the main definition of our problem and of this complication with regard to the conflicting proposals that are made toward its special formulation and toward its solution. We have now to study further the sources of insight upon which every solution of our problem must depend.

II

Our present lecture will be devoted to three tasks. First, we shall try to show that the religious consciousness of mankind, when it is concerned with the need and with the way of salvation, must needs appear in many various and apparently conflicting forms, but that, nevertheless, these conflicts need not discourage us. For, as we shall attempt still further to explain, the underlying motives of the higher religions are, after all, much more in agreement than the diversities of creeds and the apparent chaos of religious experiences would lead us to imagine. In order to make this deeper unity of the higher religious life of mankind plain, we shall try to show, more fully than we did in the last lecture, how the consciousness of the ideal of life, and of the need of salvation, naturally arises in the experience of the individual man. The religious paradox, as, in our former lecture, we defined that paradox, depends upon the fact that the principal religious motives are indeed perfectly natural and

human motives, which need no mysterious movings
from another world to explain their presence in our
lives; while, on the other hand, these very motives,
when once they appear, force us to seek for relief
from spiritual sources that cannot satisfy unless
they are far above our natural human level of life—
that is, unless they are in some definable sense
superhuman.   But about superhuman matters it is
not surprising that ignorant mortals should widely
differ, despite the deeper unity that underlies all
our nobler religious needs.

Thus the unity of the religious concerns of mankind is perfectly compatible with the fact that men
differ so widely in faith.   The mysteries of religion
belong to our natural failure to conceive readily
and to grasp adequately the religious objects.   But
our religious need is not a mystery; and our religious interests are as natural as is our ignorance.
The higher forms of the religious consciousness are
due to perfectly human motives but lead to a stubborn quest for the superhuman.   To understand
whence the higher religions get their moving principle, you have only to survey our natural life as it
is, in all its pathetic and needy fallibility.   But if
the higher religions are to find what they seek, they
call for sources of insight which you cannot define,
unless we are able to know a reality that transcends
human nature as it is—unless we can come into
genuine intercourse with a spiritual realm that is
above man.   This naturalness of the religious mo-

tives, this supernatural and naturally baffling character of the religious objects, I am, then, first to illustrate still further than I at the last time was able to do.

I shall thus be led, in the second place, to the mention of that source of religious insight to which, at the close of the former lecture, I directed your attention, namely, to our social experience. Society, in a certain sense, both includes and transcends the individual man. Perhaps, then, something can be done toward solving the problem of the religious paradox, and toward harmonising the varieties of religious opinion, by considering the religious meaning of our social consciousness. The religious paradox is that the needy and ignorant natural man must somehow obtain the spiritual power to get into a genuine touch with a real life that is above his own level. If he is to be saved, something that is divine must come to be born in the humble manger of his poor natural life. How is this apparition of the divine in the human, of the supernatural in the natural, conceivable? It is that question which most of all divides men into various religious sects. Perhaps a study of our social experience, which, indeed, often tends to mould our naturally narrow selfishness into nobler spiritual forms, may throw light upon this problem. And so I shall, in this second part of the present discourse, state the case for our social experience as a source of religious insight.

We shall, however, no sooner state this case than we shall begin to see how inadequate our ordinary social experience is to give us full religious insight. Therefore, in the third place, I shall try to estimate more critically both the merits and the imperfections of this second source of religious light, and thus I shall be led, as I close, to the mention of a third source, from which, as I hold, we can learn what neither our unaided private experience nor our ordinary social experience ever adequately shows.

III

Let me proceed at once to the first of these three undertakings. I am further to illustrate, on the one hand, the unity and the naturalness of the religious motives; on the other hand, I am to emphasise the mysterious seeming of the religious objects. And I am thus to show the reason why the faiths of men are so diverse but their religious needs so nearly common.

At the last time I tried to define for you, in my own terms, what the supreme purpose of human life is, or, in other words, what that highest good is which we are all in such peril of missing that we need salvation from this peril. My definition was this: We are naturally creatures of wavering and conflicting motives, passions, desires. The supreme aim of life is to triumph over this natural chaos, to set some one plan of life above all the others, to give

unity to our desires, to organise our activities, to
win, not, indeed, the passionless peace of Nirvana,
but the strength of spirit which is above the narrowness of each one of our separate passions. We need
to conceive of such a triumphant and unified life,
and successfully to live it. That is our goal: Self-
possession, unity, peace, and spiritual power through
and yet beyond all the turmoil of life—the victory
that overcometh in the world.

Now this definition of the ideal life will have
seemed to some of you too much a merely philosophical formula. You will say that this is not
what plain men have in mind when they ask God's
help, or lament their sins, or look to religion for
consolation.

I grant you that, since I am here concerned with
philosophy and not with preaching, I, of course,
prefer, for my present purpose, a formulation of
the ideal of life in reflective, in thoughtful terms.
But I cannot admit that plain men, in their religious moods, are not concerned with the ideal of life
which I thus reflectively formulate. I am trying to
formulate the ideal of life that seems to me to underlie all the higher religions. It is one thing,
however, to feel an interest and another thing to
become conscious of the meaning of the interest.
No matter how inarticulate may be a man's sense
of his need, that sense, if deep and genuine, may
imply a view of life which a whole system of ethics
and of metaphysics may be needed to expound.

Philosophy ought to be considerate, and to use more or less technical speech, but it need not be on that account inhuman. Its concern is with what common-sense means but does not express in clearly conscious terms. It does not want to substitute its formulas for life. It does desire to add its thoughtfulness to the intensity of life's great concerns and to enlighten us regarding what aims life has always really intended to pursue.

My own effort to formulate the supreme end of life does not seem to me to be foreign to common-sense. I think that this way of stating the purpose of life may help us to see through many of the apparently hopeless diversities of human opinion regarding what the highest good is.

It is customary to describe that longing for salvation which is, from the point of view of these lectures, the foundation of religion, by saying that the man who begins to get religious interest discovers that when left to himself he is out of harmony with what James calls "the higher powers," that is, with what a Christian calls God. In other words, as a customary formula states the case, the religiously disposed man begins by learning that the chief end of his existence is to come into harmony with God's will. And this discovery, as such a view supposes, teaches him, for the first time, what his ideal of life ought to be. And therefore, as many say, something that is of the nature of a mysterious revelation from without is needed to

initiate the religious process and to show us our
goal. On the other hand, writers like James, who
insist upon interpreting religion, so far as that
is possible, in terms of personal experience rather
than in terms of external revelation, have nevertheless been led to agree with many of the partisans of revelation in regarding this sense of our
disharmony with the "higher powers" as something that must have an essentially superhuman
source. For James, our sense of religious need is
an experience which mysteriously wells up from the
subliminal self, from the soundless depths of our
own subconsciousness. James, therefore, conceives
it probable that, through the subliminal or subconscious self, we are actually aroused to religious interest by spiritual beings whose level is higher than our
own, and whose will, expressed to us through the
vague but often intense sense of need which the
religiously minded feel, does set for us an ideal
task which is of greater worth than our natural
desires, and which, when we can get into harmony
with these powers through the aid of their subliminal influences, does give a new sense to life.

Now in contrast with such views regarding the
origin of that deeper sense of need which is indeed
the beginning of religion, I have to insist that the
basis of the religious interest is something much
less mysterious than James's supposed workings of
the "higher powers" through our subliminal selves,
and is also something much more universally human

than is the opportunity to come under the influence
of any one revelation. Men who never heard of
Christianity, and men who have never felt conscious of any external revelation from above, as
well as men who have had no such sudden uprushes
from their own subconscious natures as James's
"religious geniuses" have reported, are able to win
a genuine religious interest, to be aware of an intense
need for salvation, and to set before themselves, in
however inarticulate a fashion, the very ideal of life
which I have been trying in my own way to formulate. The need and the ideal can come into sight
in a manner that indeed does not in the least either
exclude or require a belief in one or in another
reported revelation, but that links both the need
and the ideal to our ordinary personal experience
by ties which are not at all mysterious. Let me
show you, then, better than my time permitted in
the former lecture, how an individual may naturally experience what I have called his need of salvation.

Nothing is more obvious about the natural course
of our lives than is the *narrowness* of view to which
we are usually subject. We are not only the victims
of conflicting motives, but we are often too narrow
to know that this is true. For we see our various
life interests, so to speak, one at a time. We forget
one while we are living out another. And so we are
prone to live many lives, seldom noting how ill
harmonised they are. Home life, for instance, may

be one thing; business life in principle another; sport or social ambition another. And these various lives may be lived upon mutually inconsistent plans. We forget one part of ourselves in our temporary absorption in some other part. And if, as our naturally complex and often conflicting motives determine, these our various lives are out of harmony with one another, we constantly do irrevocable deeds that emphasise and perpetuate the results of this disharmony. And as we grow older our motives alter; yet because of our natural narrowness of interest, we often do not recognise the change. Our youth consequently lays a poor foundation for our age; or perhaps our mature life makes naught of the aspirations of our youth. We thus come to spend a great part of our days thwarting ourselves through the results of our fickleness, yet without knowing who it is that thwarts us. We love, and, like Siegfried, forget our former beloved, and perhaps live to feel the fatal spear-thrust that avenges our treason to our own past. The deeper tragedies of life largely result from this our narrowness of view.

But over against this narrowness of our ordinary activities there, indeed, stand certain moments when we get a wider vision of ourselves, when we review life, or foresee it with a broad outlook. These are, indeed, moments of insight. We all know how tragic they often are, because they show us at a glance how with the left hand we have undone the

right hand's work, how we have loved and forgotten, how we have sworn fealty to many masters,
and have cheated one while we served another,
how absorption in business has made us unworthy of
home, or how we have wantonly sacrificed a friend in
order to win a game, or gained our bit of the world
through what, upon review, we have to call the loss
of our souls. Such moments of insight come to us
sometimes when our friends die, and when memory
reminds us of our neglected debts of love or of
gratitude to them, or when worldly defeat reawakens
the long-forgotten unworldly aspirations that we
abandoned in order to do what has ended in earn-
ing the defeat. These are, I repeat, often tragic
moments. But they enlighten. And they show us
our need. And they arise as naturally as does any
other incident of a reasonable life.

What need do they show? I answer, the need to
possess what by mere nature we never come to
possess, namely, the power to "see life steadily and
see it whole," and then to live triumphantly in the
light of this vision. Can a plain man who is no
philosopher feel this need? I answer, Yes, whenever he has his moments of vision; whenever he
feels the longing for the clean, straight, unswerving
will, for the hearty whole life; whenever he sees
and regrets his fickleness, just because it means
self-defeat; whenever he seeks to be true to himself. At such moment his highest aim is the aim
that there should be a highest aim in life, and that

this aim should win what it seeks. He has the longing, however inarticulate, for integrity of spirit and for success in winning the fruits of integrity.

When the plain man feels what I venture thus to formulate, how will he express his longing? He will, of course, not use my present formulas. He will seize upon whatever expressions the creed or the language of his tribe may suggest to him. He may say, and perhaps truthfully: "This is the ideal that God sets before me. This is the divine will regarding my life." For at such times he conceives of God as the being who has widest vision and who knows him best. Therefore he conceives of God's plan as the fulfilment of his own rational plan. But the interior source of the plain man's view regarding the divine will is simply his better vision of the meaning of his life, the vision that comes at moments when he is not forgetful of the whole; when he does not want to swear fidelity to one beloved, and then, like Siegfried, pursue and win another; when he wants to be true to the whole of himself. No wonder that he, indeed, conceives this supreme goal of life as the goal set for him by some will higher than his own private will. He is right. For, as we shall see, throughout our later study, we are, indeed, helpless either to hold before us this our personal vision of the triumphant life and of the unity of the spirit, or to turn the vision into a practical reality, unless we come into touch and keep in touch with an order of spiritual existence which is in a perfectly genuine sense superhuman, and in the same sense supernatural, and which certainly is not our natural selves.

But in any case the plain man must needs interpret his vision of the ideal in terms of whatever conception of God, or of the triumphant life, or of spiritual power, his traditions and his stage of personal development may suggest to him. Hence the endless varieties in the formulation of the religious ideal. Whatever is suggested to a man, at his moments of wider vision, as a law or as a motive which, *if* it were the ruling motive or the supreme law would make life a consistent whole—this he takes to be God's will, or the truth that is to save him if, indeed, salvation is possible.

If this account of the sources of the religious motive is right, we need not view the religious interest as the result of an arbitrary intrusion from above—as if the gods loved to disturb us and to trouble our peace. Nor need we, with James, speak of a marvellous and capricious uprush from below the level of our natural consciousness. Yet just as little need we think of religion as having no concern with what is, indeed, superhuman. Religion is, indeed, our own affair; for it grows out of our personal vision of the transformation that a divinely enlarged power to comprehend, to survey, to harmonise, to triumph over our natural life would give. This vision comes to us at moments, in glimpses—and is seen through a glass darkly. Our

need is to see face to face and to live in the light
thus to be discovered. And so to live would be
salvation. The word salvation is fitting, because
the need is so great and because the transformation
would be so profound. The endlessly various interpretations of this one ideal and of the nature of the
saving process are due to the wealth of life and to
the imposing multitude of motives and of experiences that the religious consciousness has to consider. But beneath and above all the varieties of
religious experience lies the effort to win in reality
what the vision of the harmonious and triumphant
life suggests to us in our moments of clearness.
Since our own natures leave us hopelessly remote
from this goal, while our glimpses of spiritual harmony and power reveal to us its preciousness, our
religious need is supreme, and is accompanied with
the perfectly well-warranted assurance that we cannot attain the goal unless we can get into some sort
of communion with a real life infinitely richer than
our own—a life that is guided by a perfect and
unwavering vision, and that somehow conquers and
annuls all fickleness, conflict, and estrangement.
Such a life rightly seems to us to be superhuman
in its breadth of view and in its spiritual power, if
indeed there be such a life at all. If there is no
such life, none the less we need it, and so need
salvation. If salvation is possible, then there is in
the universe some being that knows us, and that is
the master of life. And we seek ourselves to know

even as we are known and to live as the wise one
would have us live.

Thus simple and, for all to whom even the occasional moments of wider vision come, universal are
the religious motives. James was wrong when he
sought them in any capricious interference of the
subliminal self, or of its superhuman controls, with
our natural selves. It is we who in our natural
lives are capricious and narrowly interfere with
our own freedom. It is we who are the disturbers
of our own peace. The religious ideal grows out
of the vision of a spiritual freedom and peace which
are not naturally ours. No two of us get that vision
in quite the same way. But all its forms show us
the same far-off shining light. The problem of
religious insight is the problem whether that light
is a mirage.

No wonder, then, that men differ as to their special
efforts to solve such a problem. But it is now our
task to seek for further sources of insight.

IV

The foregoing discussion may seem to have led
us far from the study of our social experience as a
source of religious insight. But in fact it is a necessary preliminary to that study and leads us very
near to it.

If one principal source of our need of salvation is
the natural narrowness of our view of the meaning

of our own purposes and motives, and the consequent fickleness and the forgetful inconsistency with which we usually live out our days, it seems right, in searching for a way that may lead toward salvation, to get such help as we can by looking to our normal social experience for whatever guidance it can give. The social world is wide, even if it is still full of conflict. It broadens our outlook at every turn. A man corrects his own narrowness by trying to share his fellow's point of view. Our social responsibilities tend to set limits to our fickleness. Social discipline removes some of our inner conflicts, by teaching us not to indulge caprices. Human companionship may calm, may steady our vision, may bring us into intercourse with what is in general much better than a man's subliminal self, namely, his public, his humane, his greater social self, wherein he finds his soul and its interests writ large. Perhaps, then, whatever the ultimate goal, the way out of the distractions of the natural self, the way toward the divine insight and power that we need, lies through our social experience.

No wonder, then, that in the religious discussions of to-day our social experience is that source of insight upon which a great number of our teachers, whether they are professional religious teachers or not, most frequently insist. Our present time is an age of great concern with social problems and reforms. No wonder, then, that we have all learned to widen our vision, and to control our waywardness, by remembering that man is a being who can be neither understood nor directed in case you try to view him in isolation. As for salvation, many of our most influential leaders now teach us that the problem of our day is the problem of saving, not the individual as an individual, but the social order as a whole. The two tendencies which seem to be most potent in the political realm are the general tendencies known by the admittedly vague names of democracy and socialism. Solidarity, collectivism, the common life—these are the watchwords of some of the most widely influential movements of our time.

And these watchwords have, for many of us, not only a political, but a religious meaning. I need not remind you of the popular influence of such dramas as "The Servant in the House," or of the numbers of clergymen to whom the preaching of religion has come to mean, in the main, the preaching of beneficent social reforms. If teachers who thus view religion as, on the whole, a movement toward the increase of social welfare are asked what their counsel is to the individual regarding the salvation of his soul, they will reply: "If you want to be saved, come out of yourself." Some of them would add: "Forget yourself." But whether they use this latter extremely ambiguous and doubtful form of advice, they very generally agree that to seek to save your own soul by any merely or mainly inward and non-social process is to secure perdition. "It is love that saves," they are fond of telling us. And in this doctrine, as interpreted in the light of our modern social movements, many see the entire essence of Christianity adapted to our present situation.

Nor is the tendency here in question limited to the practical counsels of which I have just reminded you. There are those students of the psychology and the philosophy of religion who are disposed to conceive that the whole essence of the religion of all times, the entire meaning of religious beliefs and practices, can be exhaustively and accurately described in the purely human and social terms which these practical counsels attempt to embody. A recent writer on the psychology of religion defines religion as man's consciousness of his highest social values, and maintains that all religious beliefs are attempts to express this consciousness in whatever terms a given stage of civilisation makes natural and possible.

One can easily suggest to any student of general history some of the facts which such a writer has in mind. Have not the gods often been conceived as tribal deities, and so simply as representatives of the welfare and of the will of the community over against the waywardness and the capriciousness of the individual? Was not the transition from polytheism to the various forms of pantheism and of monotheism determined by the social processes that formed kingdoms or empires, and that finally led over to the modern appreciation of the value of the

common interest of an ideally united humanity?
Were not the prophets of Israel social reformers?
Was not the work of Jesus an anticipation and a
prophecy of the coming consciousness of the brotherhood of man, as the lovers of mankind now conceive that brotherhood? What has religion had to
teach us, some will insistently ask, more saving,
unifying, sustaining, than this love of man for man?

From such a point of view, as you see, our social
experience is our principal source of religious insight.
And the salvation that this insight brings to our
knowledge is salvation through the fostering of
human brotherhood. Such salvation accrues to the
individual so far as he gives himself over to the
service of man, and to mankind in so far as men
can only be saved together and not separately.

I am just now depicting, not judging, a view concerning the solution of religious problems which
you know to be, in our day, as potent as it is varied
and problematic in its teaching. Can this view
satisfy? Does this way of stating the case really
indicate to us any adequate source of religious
insight, any way in which we can define the true
salvation of man?

V

We cannot answer this question without taking
account of the views of those of our recent teachers
to whom this purely social theory of the religious

objects and values is indeed profoundly unsatisfactory. That such opponents of the adequacy of
the interpretation of religion just suggested are to
be found amongst the believers in familiar religious traditions, we need not at any length set forth.
The traditions of the great religions of the world
do not interpret the old faiths in this way, just
because these religious traditions all agree in regarding the human social order as something which
exists for the sake of an essentially superhuman
order. As these various faiths assert, man can
never be saved by purely human means, whether
you call these means preventive medicine, or socialism, or universal brotherhood, or even love, so long
as love means simply human love. As for Christianity, in all its older forms, it has emphasised
the love of man, but always in a certain union with
the love of God which tradition could never conceive as adequately expressible in terms of our
recent social movements. The "Servant in the
House" is supposed to be a modern apparition of
the Christ; but he is explicitly a heretic regarding
the old faith of the church.

But with tradition as tradition, these lectures
have to do only by way of occasional illustration.
What interests us more, for our present purpose, is
the fact that, despite the predominance of the social
interpretations of religion of which I have just
reminded you, there are still some of our recent
teachers who stoutly insist that our social experi-

ence does not adequately show us any way of salvation whatever.

And here first I must call attention to certain of the most modern and least theologically disposed of our leaders, namely, to those who emphasise the most characteristic recent forms of individualism. I have mentioned Nietzsche in my former lecture. Surely he stands for opposition to tradition and he expresses tendencies that are potent to-day. But while he lived and wrote, he aspired to be a sort of Antichrist, and preached the doctrine that a religion of love can never save, because, as he insists, what the self needs is power, and power is not to be won by attempting to please a world of slaves. Nietzsche may seem to you, as he has seemed to so many, a hopeless abnormity; but his Titanism is in fact a wayward modern expression of a motive that has always played its notable part in the search for salvation, ever since heroism and the resolute will were first discovered by man. Nietzsche's insight too, such as it is, is a social insight. It comes through noting that, even if the individual needs his social world as a means of grace and a gateway to salvation, the social order, in its turn, needs individuals that are worth saving, and can never be saved unless it expresses itself through the deeds and the inner life of souls deeply conscious of the dignity of selfhood, of the infinite worth of unique and intensely conscious personal life.

As a fact, individualism is as potent an ethical motive in the life of to-day as is the collectivism just characterised. Each of these tendencies, in our present social order, feeds upon and intensifies the other. Socialism opposes, and yet inevitably encourages, the purposes of the very individual who feels his social ties as a galling restraint. It preaches solidarity and brotherhood and love; but wins a ready hearing from those who view all these tendencies mainly as means whereby they may hope to have their own way, and to become, as Nietzsche's Superman, "beyond good and evil"— masters in the coming world of triumphant democracy. The social experience of our time is full of ambiguous lessons. Its way toward salvation leads not only over the Hill of Difficulty, but both ways around the hill; and it shows us no one straight and narrow road to peace. Whoever would traverse its wilderness and reach salvation needs to supplement his social insight by a use of other and deeper sources.

And as to what these deeper sources of insight are, the teacher whom I have already repeatedly cited—William James—asserts a doctrine that, as you already know, I do not regard as adequate, but that I must again here emphasise, because its contrast with that social theory of religion which I just characterised is so instructive.

James, in his "Varieties of Religious Experience," shows the utmost liberality toward differences of faith, and insists in the opening chapters of his book that religious experience is a field where one must beware of defining sharp boundary lines or of showing a false exclusiveness. Yet *one* boundary line he himself defines with the greatest sharpness; and in respect of *one* matter he is rigidly exclusive. Religious experience, he insists, is, as you will remember from our first lecture, the experience of an individual who feels himself to be "alone with the divine." And the social types of religious experience James rigidly excludes from the "varieties" whereof he takes account. And James's reason for this procedure is explicit. In its social aspects religion, so he insists, always becomes, or has already become, conventional. James no longer finds in the religious life of communities the novelty and independence of vision which he prizes. The essence of true religious experience lies, for him, in its originality, in its spontaneity, and so in the very solitude which is a condition, to James's mind, for the discovery of that which saves.

The words "originality" and "spontaneity" emphasise the features which, as I think, James most meant to emphasise. The problem of salvation, for James, must be an essentially individual problem; for nobody else ever faced *your* need of salvation, or had your personal issues to meet. If you win religious insight, you will have to win it very much as you will have to die—alone. Of course James does not hesitate to test the value of religious experience, in his pragmatic fashion, by its social as well as by its individual consequences. The fruits of the spirit accrue to the general advantage; and the saint, in James's opinion, must indeed undertake to edify, not only himself, but also his brethren. But the effects of religious insight must not be confused with the sources. James insists that the sources are mainly from within the individual and are only incidentally social. A religious discovery has in common with a poetic creation the fact that the religious genius, like the artist, sees his vision, and produces his spiritual miracle, in solitude.

If you ask whether this position which James assumes is anything more than his own private opinion, and if you want to know his grounds for it, a closer examination of his book will show you why he thus deliberately turns his back upon the favourite recent interpretation of religion as an essentially social phenomenon. James, in common with the traditional faiths, although not in conformity with their formulas, always conceived religious experience as an intercourse with objects and with powers that, whatever their deeper bases in our "subliminal" nature, do not adequately express themselves in our everyday, worldly, overt human nature. And in our social life, where the conventional reigns, where man imitates man or contends with man, where crowds bustle and the small-talk or the passionate struggle of the day fill the mind, where lovers pursue their beloved and are jealous of their rivals, and laborers toil and sweat, and worldly authorities display their pomp, you meet not the solution, but the problem of life. James, as man, was full of social interests, and, as psychologist, was fond of studying social processes. But when a man wants peace and spiritual triumph, James observes that, as an empirical fact, he does not readily find them in the market-place, or on the battle-field, or in the law courts, unless, indeed, he comes to these places already full of the light that the saintly souls have often found in the wilderness or in their meditations. In brief, James always emphasises the mystical element in religious experience and is full of the assurance that religion cannot find its food in the commonplace; while our social life is a realm where the commonplace holds sway. Or again, James holds that when the faithful have thought of their religious experience as an intercourse with beings of a level wholly superhuman, they may, indeed, have been wrong in their creeds, but were right in holding that man as he lives in his social world can never save man. Our social consciousness is too barefaced and open in its union of triviality and pathos. What we want as the saving power is, for a teacher such as James, something more mysterious, deep, subconscious or superconscious, and in this sense, indeed, superhuman.

Still I am only depicting, not yet judging. I have now briefly stated opinions that favour and opinions that oppose an interpretation of religious insight in terms of our social experience. But what are the merits of the case? In what sense can there be a religion of the social consciousness?

VI

The answer to this question involves, I think, two considerations, both of them exemplified by the various views here in question, both of them familiar, both of them easily misinterpreted. The first is the very consideration upon which our popular teachers of salvation through love most insist. We ourselves came upon that consideration at the close of our first lecture. Man is, indeed, a being who cannot be saved alone, however much solitude may help him, at times, toward insight. For he is bound to his brethren by spiritual links that cannot be broken. The second consideration is this: So long as man views his fellow-man *merely* as fellow-man, he only complicates his problem, for both he and his fellow equally need salvation. Their plight is common; their very need of salvation chains them together in the prison of human sorrow. If, to adapt the symbolism of ancient stories to our case, the angel of love is to appear in their prison, is to loosen their chains, is to open the doors, it must be, in some wise, as an angel, not as a merely human presence, that love must appear.

Perhaps the best way to indicate wherein lies the

strength and the weakness, the irresistible authority
and the pathetic limitation of our social experience
as a religious guide, and the best way also to indicate its true relations to the religious experience of
the human individual, is to remind ourselves of a
very few familiar cases in which an individual finds
that his own way toward salvation, if any such way
is to exist for him at all, lies through his social
world, so that he cannot be saved without the help
of his fellows.

Our first instance shall be an extreme one, in
which the sense of need is intense and the longing
for salvation acute, but where there is little or no
hope of finding the way, although one knows that
if the way could be found it would bring one into
touch with a new type of human companionship.
We all know how the sense of guilt may take the
form of a feeling of overwhelming loneliness. Now
the sense of guilt, if deep and pervasive and passionate, involves at least a dim recognition that there
is some central aim of life and that one has come
hopelessly short of that aim. I may regret a blunder,
and yet have no hint that there is any unified and
supreme ideal of life. For a blunder is a special
affair involving the missing of some particular aim.
I may even bitterly repent a fault, and still think
of that fault as a refusal to pursue some one separate
moral purpose—a violation of this or of that maxim
of conduct. But the true sense of guilt in its
greater manifestation involves a confession that the

whole self is somehow tainted, the whole life, for the time being, wrecked. But the bankruptcy of the self implies that there is one highest purpose which gives the self its value; the sense of total failure is itself a revelation of the value of what was lost. Hence the highly idealising tendency of the great experiences of moral suffering. They lead us to think not of this or of that special good, but of salvation and perdition in their general bearing upon life. The depth of the despair shows the grandeur of what has been missed; and it is therefore not surprising that experiences of this sort have been, for so many, the beginnings of religious insight. To believe that one is cut off from salvation may be the very crisis that in the end saves.

Now some of those who feel this overmastering might of their guilt lay most stress upon their assurance that God has condemned them. And religious tradition has of course emphasised this way of stating the case. But it is perfectly natural, and is surely a humane experience, to feel the sense of guilt primarily in the form of a belief that one is an outcast from human sympathy and is hopelessly alone. The more abnormal types of the sense of guilt, in nervous patients, frequently exemplify this terror of the lonely soul, this inner grief over the homelessness of the remorseful outcast. But actual guilt may be present with or without the more abnormal nervous conditions just mentioned, and, when present, may bring home to the rueful mind the despair of the awakened but forsaken sinner, and may bring it in the form of the feeling of guilty solitude.

A well-known expression of such a mood you find in Kipling's lyric of the "Poor little sheep that have gone astray." In these verses the outcast sons of good families, the "gentlemen-rankers," dwell together in an agonised companionship of common loneliness. Their guilt and their lost homes are for them inseparably associated.

Or again: Beneath all the fantastic imagery of Coleridge's "Ancient Mariner," the poet uses a perfectly recognisable type of the sense of guilt as the means to make his tale of wonders seem, despite all its impossibilities, human and even plausible. The incidents are the miracles of a magic dream; but the human nature depicted is as real as is the torment of any guilty conscience. Somehow—no matter how, or under how arbitrary conditions— the hero has committed a crime without precisely intending it to be a crime. His tale is one of a young man's adventurous insolence. His deed has all the too familiar characters of the typical sins of wayward youth. And that is why the gay young wedding guest must hear his tale. He—the mariner— in his own youth, had consciously meant to be only a little wanton and cruel. He awakened, as many a light-minded youth later awakes, to find that, as a fact, he had somehow struck at the very centre of life, at the heart of love, at the laws that bind the

world together, at the spirit of the universe. When
one thus awakes, he sees that nature and God are
against him. But, worst of all, he has become a
curse to his fellows; and in turn they curse him;
and then they leave him alone with the nightmare
life in death of utter solitude. To his mind there
are no living men. He sees about him only "the
curse in a dead man's eye." What life he can still
see is no longer, to his morbid eyes, really human:

> "The many men, so beautiful!
>   And they all dead did lie;
>   And a thousand, thousand slimy things
>   Lived on; and so did I."

The Ancient Mariner's escape from the horrors of
this despair, the beginnings of his salvation, date
from the first movings of love in his heart toward
all living beings. His salvation is won when, at
the end, he finds God along with the goodly company at the kirk. In brief, the curse of his guilt
is to be "alone on a wide, wide sea." His salvation
comes in preaching love and companionship, and in
uniting himself hereby to the God who loves all
things both great and small.

Now one does not often think of the "Ancient
Mariner" as a poem of religious experience; but
apart from its brilliant play with natural magic,
its human charm actually depends upon this well-
founded picture of the loneliness of guilt and of the
escape through loving union with one's kind. And

the poet deliberately gives to this picture the form
and the sense of a religious process of salvation.

If you turn from the dreamy product of Coleridge's youthful fancy to the opposite pole of modern
literature, you find an instance of almost the same
motives at the basis of that most impressive romance
of the Russian Dostoieffsky: "Crime and Punishment." Dostoieffsky had himself lived long in
what he called "The House of the Dead," in Siberia,
before he learned how to write this masterpiece.
He had been forced to sojourn amongst the guilty
of the most various grades. He had come to universalise their experiences and to struggle himself
with one form of the problem of salvation. Those
who, like Dante, have looked upon hell, sometimes
have, indeed, wonders to tell us. Dostoieffsky con-
denses the whole problem of salvation from guilt
in this picture of an individual. Raskolnikow, the
hero, after his thoughtfully conceived crime, and
after his laborious effort at self-justification, finds
himself the prey of a simply overwhelming sense
that he walks alone amongst men, and that, in the
crowded streets of the city, he is as one dead amongst
spectres. There is nowhere, I think, a more persuasive picture of the loneliness of great guilt.
Raskolnikow could not be more the victim of supernatural forces if he were Coleridge's Ancient Mariner. Like the Ancient Mariner, Raskolnikow in
the end finds the way to salvation through love—
the love which the martyred Sonia teaches him—

herself, as our Russian most persuasively pictures
her, at once outcast and saint. The author uses
religious conceptions which are both ancient and,
in his use of them, unconventional. But the central one of these is the familiar conception that
salvation involves a reconciliation both with the
social and with the divine order, a reconciliation
through love and suffering—an escape from the
wilderness of lonely guilt to the realm where men
can understand one another.

In such elemental ways the process of salvation
can be made to appear as essentially a social process,
just because its opposite, perdition, seems to mean
banishment from amongst men.

Another group of cases presents to us the same
need for human companionship as a means to salvation, but presents it in the winning guise of salvation beginning through love, without the main
stress being laid upon the previous despair. In
such cases the despair may be mentioned but at
once relieved. The religion of friendship and of
love is a familiar human experience. James, in his
fear of debasing religion by romantic or by grosser
associations, unjustly neglects it in his study of
"varieties." In fact, to seem to find the divine in
the person of your idealised friend or beloved is a
perfectly normal way of beginning your acquaintance with the means of grace. You meet, you
love, and—you seem to be finding God. Or, to
use our present interpretation of what reveals the

divine, love seems to furnish you with a vision of a
perfect life, to give you a total survey of the sense
of your own life, and to begin to show you how to
triumph. If there be any divine life, you say, this
is my vision of its beauty and its harmony. So
the divine appears in one of Browning's later
lyrics:

> "Such a starved bank of moss,
>   Till, that May morn,
> Blue ran the flash across;
>   Violets were born!

> "Sky—what a scowl of cloud
>   Till, near and far,
> Ray on ray split the shroud
>   Splendid! a star!

> "World—how it walled about
>   Life with disgrace,
> Till God's own smile came out;
>   That was thy face!"

In the sonnets of Shakespeare this religion of
friendship has found some of its most perfect
expressions.

> "Haply I think of thee, and then my state,
>   Like to the lark's, at break of day arising
> From sullen earth, sings hymns at heaven's gate."

And again, in Mrs. Browning's "Sonnets from the
Portuguese," the religion of love not only uses
speech intensely personal, fond, intimate, but also,

and deliberately, accompanies all this with words derived from reflective metaphysics, or from theology, and intended to express the miracle that the nearest movings of affection are also a revelation of the highest powers of the spiritual world.

> "How do I love thee? Let me count the ways.
>   I love thee to the depth and breadth and height
>   My soul can reach, when feeling out of sight
> For the ends of Being, and Ideal Grace.
> I love thee to the level of everyday's
>   Most quiet need, by sun and candle light.
>   I love thee freely, as men strive for Right;
> I love thee purely, as they turn from Praise;
>   I love thee with the passion put to use
> In my old griefs, and with my childhood's faith;
>   I love thee with a love I seemed to lose
> With my lost saints,—I love thee with the breath,
>   Smiles, tears, of all my life!—and, if God choose,
> I shall but love thee better after death."

Surely one could not better express, than this sonnet does, the naturalness of the religious motive—the mystery of the religious object.

And finally, turning from these cases to those which are social in the larger sense, every patriotic song which deifies one's country, every other form of the religion of patriotism, exemplifies the experience of the devoted lover of his country by teaching that it is "man's perdition to be safe" in case his social world calls for the sacrifice of his life, and that salvation comes through service.

James is indeed wrong then to neglect the social roads that lead toward the experience of what one takes to be divine. There is no love so simpleminded that, if it be true love, the way of salvation may not seem to be opened through it to the lover.

But observe that, as we review these instances, they show us how the social world wherein they bid us seek our salvation is a world whose very essence is transformed by love and by its vision into something that seems to the lover mystical, superhuman, and more than our literal and commonplace social life directly exemplifies. Those who have failed to find in their actual social life such inspirations may, indeed, have to look, as the typical mystics have generally done, elsewhere, for their vision of the divine, than in so much of the social world as they know. And such will, indeed, seek their vision of salvation in solitude. When they tell us of their experience, they may well remind the social enthusiast, as well as the lover, that the religion of love is no religion at all, unless it conceives its human object not only as this creature, or as this collection of needy men and women, but as a hint, or revelation, or incarnation of a divine process—of a process which is not only human but superhuman, and which can never be comprehended in the "mart and the crowded street" unless by the soul that is either mystical enough to meet God also "in the bush," or rationally enlightened enough to know that human life is indeed a revelation of something that is also superhuman.

I conclude, then, for the moment, thus: Social experience seems to lie on the way to salvation. Normally the way to salvation, if there be any such way, must lead through social experience. But when our social experience shows us any such way upward it does so, if it truly does so, because human social life is the hint, the likeness, or the incarnation of a life that lies beyond and above our present human existence. For human society as it now is, in this world of care, is a chaos of needs; and the whole social order groans and travails together in pain until now, longing for salvation. It can be saved, as the individual can be saved, only in case there is some way that leads upward, through all our turmoil and our social bickerings, to a realm where that vision of unity and self-possession which our clearest moments bring to us becomes not merely vision, but fulfilment, where love finds its own, and where the power of the spirit triumphs. Of such a realm the lovers dream and the religions tell. Let us appeal to a further source of insight. Concerning the realities that we need, let us next consult our Reason.

III

THE OFFICE OF THE REASON

III

THE OFFICE OF THE REASON

Thus far we have dealt with sources of religious insight which are indispensable, but which confess their own inadequacy so soon as you question them closely. Individual experience can show us, in its moments of wider vision, our ideal, and its times of despair, of aspiration, or of self-examination, our need. But whenever it attempts to acquaint us with the way of salvation, its deliveries are clouded by the mists of private caprice and of personal emotion. Social experience, in its religious aspects, helps the individual to win the wider outlook, helps him also to find his way out of the loneliness of guilt and of failure toward wholeness of life, and promises salvation through love. But, like individual experience, it is beset by what we have called the religious paradox. And it does not solve that paradox. Confessing its own defects, it still undertakes to discern how to overcome them. In so far as it is merely social experience it deals with the world of weak mortals, of futile bickerings, and of love that, in this world, deifies but never quite finds its true beloved. By virtue of this transforming love it indeed gives us the hint that our social world may be an apparition or an incarnation of some diviner life than any mortal now experiences. Yet how can mortals thus ignorant pretend to get insight into anything that is divinely exalted?

Thus, both the sources of insight that we have thus far consulted point beyond themselves. Each says, "If salvation is possible, then human life must be able to come into touch with a life whose meaning is superhuman." Our question is: "Is there, indeed, such a diviner life?" In order to deal with this question, we have resolved to consult still another source of insight, namely, our Reason. The present lecture must deal with this source of insight.

I

"What does one mean by the Reason?" As I attempt to answer this question, with an especial effort to show the relations of reason and religion, I shall be aided by reminding you at the outset that, at the present time, there is a widespread tendency to discredit the reason as a source of any notable insight into life or into the universe. And this tendency depends upon so defining the business of the reason as sharply to oppose, on the one hand, intuition and reason, and, on the other hand, reason and common-sense experience. That is, some of our recent teachers tell us that the only sort of insight which can be of any use in religion must be

won by intuitions and cannot be obtained by what
these teachers call the abstract reason. By intuition, at least in the religious field, such men mean
some sort of direct feeling of the nature of things,
some experience such as the mystics have reported,
or such as many religious people, whether technical
mystics or not, call illumination through faith. Intuitions of this sort, they say, are our only guides in
the religious field. As opposed to such direct apprehension, the use of reason would mean the effort
to be guided by formulas, by explicitly stated abstract principles, by processes of inference, by cal-
culations, or by logical demonstrations. James is
prominent amongst those who thus oppose the abstract reason to the revelations of intuition; and,
especially in his later works, he is never weary of
emphasising the inarticulate character of all our
deepest sources of religious insight. When we get
true religious insight, so he teaches, we simply feel
convinced that these things are so. If we try to
give reasons for our beliefs, James holds that the
reasons are inapt afterthoughts, the outcome of
sophistication, or are at best useful only in putting
our convictions into convenient order for purposes
of record or of teaching. James's favourite statement of the contrast here in question identifies the
partisans of reason with the defenders of what he
calls "barren intellectualism." He maintains that
religion is hindered rather than helped by such
people. You attain conviction by processes of

which the "barren intellect" can give no adequate account. Conviction, in religious matters, emanates, according to James, from those mysterious depths of the subconscious about which I said something in the last lecture. And convictions thus resulting feel overwhelming to the persons who have them. Such convictions are what many denote by the word "intuitions." The effort to define abstract principles, as grounds for holding your convictions to be true, constitutes the only effort of the reason in religious matters which James recognises. According to James, such reasoning processes are inevitably bad. And as a fact, so he insists, nobody seriously believes in God because some theologian or philosopher pretends to have demonstrated his existence. On the contrary, he says, belief in God is intuitive or is nothing of value. And reason is employed in such matters merely because of a frequent overfondness for abstract conceptions, or at best because formulas are useful for the teachers of religious traditions.

Another form of contrast, and one upon which James also often insists, while many other recent writers, whose interests are not those of James, emphasise the same matter, depends upon opposing reason to experience in general, including under the latter term not only the intuitions of the devout, but whatever goes by the name experience in ordinary speech. We see and hear and touch, and by such means get experience. But we make hypotheses and deduce their consequences; we assume premises and demonstrate conclusions; and, according to such writers, what we then do constitutes the typical work of our reason. The characteristic of the reason is that it attempts either to elucidate the meaning of an assertion, or to prove some proposition to be true, without appealing to experience to verify the proposition in question. And such work of the reason, as these writers tell us, is of very limited use, in comparison to the use of our direct experience as a guide. What is found to be true through empirical tests is rightly tested. What is supposed to be proved true by abstract reasoning is thus at best made dependent for its explicit warrant upon the presupposed truth of the premises used in the reasoning process. Or, as is sometimes said, the reason can discover nothing essentially new. It turns its premises over and over, and gets out of them only what has already been put into them. Experience, on the other hand, is full of countless novelties; for what you can find through observation and experiment depends not upon previous assumptions, but upon the skill and the good fortune of the inquirer, and upon the wealth of life and of the real world.

In brief, for those who look at reason in this way, to use your reason is simply to draw necessary inferences from assumed premises. And no premises, as such writers insist, can warrant any inference except the inference of a conclusion which is already hidden away, so to speak, in the premises themselves.

Thus reasoning, as they tell us, is a process which, in the conclusion inferred, merely lets out of the bag the cat which was concealed in that bag, namely, in the premises. Reason, therefore, is indeed (so such writers assert) barren wherever novelty is sought. It is useful only for purposes of formulation, and in certain parts of the abstract sciences, where deduction has a technical place, as a means for preparing the way for experimental tests. In life, experience is the guide to true novelty. And therefore, if religious insight can be attained at all, it must be due not to the reason, but to some sort of religious experience.

Such objections to the use of reason in the religious field depend, as you see, upon identifying the reasoning process with the combination of two well-known mental processes; first, the process of forming and using abstract conceptions; secondly, the process of analysing assertions, or combinations of assertions, to make more explicit what is already contained in their meaning. Our next question may well be this: Is such an account of the work of reason just to the actual usage that common-sense is accustomed to make of this familiar name?

II

To this question I must at once answer that we all of us daily use the word reason as the name for a process, or a set of processes, which certainly cannot be reduced to the mere power to form and to use abstract ideas, and to analyse the already predetermined meaning of statements. When we speak of an ill-tempered or of a prejudiced man as "unreasonable," we do not merely mean that he is unable to form or to define abstract ideas, or that he cannot analyse the meaning of his own statements. For sometimes such a man is contentiously thoughtful, and fond of using too many one-sided abstractions, and eager to argue altogether too vehemently. No, when we call him unreasonable, we mean that he takes a narrow view of his life, or of his duties, or of the interests of his fellow-men. We mean, in brief, that he lacks vision for the true relations and for the total values of things. When we try to correct this sort of unreasonableness, we do not say to the petulant or to the one-sided man: "Go to the dictionary, and learn how to define your abstract terms." Sometimes contentiously prejudiced men are altogether too fond of the dictionary. Nor do we merely urge him to form the habit of analysis. No, we may indeed say to him: "Be reasonable"; but we mean: "Take a wider outlook; see things not one at a time, but many at once; be broad; consider more than one side; bring your ideas together; in a word, get insight." For precisely what I defined in my opening lecture as insight is what we have in mind when, in such cases, we counsel a man to be reasonable. So, in such uses of the word reason, reason is not opposed to intuition, as the power to

form abstract ideas is supposed by James to be opposed to the power to see things by direct vision.
No, reason, in such cases, means simply broader intuition, the sort of seeing that grasps many views
in one, that surveys life as it were from above, that
sees, as the wanderer views the larger landscape
from a mountain top.

When, not long since, in a famous decision, the
Supreme Court of the United States called attention
to what it called "The rule of reason," and declared
its intention to judge the workings of well-known
modern business methods by that rule, the court certainly did not mean by "the rule of reason" the requirement that acts said to be "in restraint of
trade" must be judged merely through a process of
forming abstract ideas or of analysing the signifi-
cation of assertions. No, the court was explicitly
opposing certain methods of estimate which it regarded as falsely abstract; and it proposed to substitute for these false abstractions a mode of judging
the workings of certain trade combinations which
was to involve taking as wide and concrete and practical a view as possible of their total effects. Everybody who read the court's words understood that, in
this case, it was precisely the merely abstract conception of something technically defined as a "restraint of trade" which the court wished, not to
make sovereign, but to subordinate to the wider intuition of a fair-minded observer of the whole result, of a given sort of corporate combination. The

"rule of reason" was intended to bring the whole question out of the realm of barren abstractions and of mere analysis, and nearer to the realm where the trained observation of the fair minded man would decide the case—nearer, in fact, to the realm of intuition. Only, the decisive intuition must be something broad, and far-seeing, and synthetic, and fair.

Now I submit that this meaning of the word reason is perfectly familiar to all of you. Reason, from this point of view, is the power to see widely and steadily and connectedly. Its true opponent is not intuition, but whatever makes us narrow in outlook, and consequently the prey of our own caprices. The unreasonable person is the person who can see but one thing at a time, when he ought to see two or many things together; who can grasp but one idea, when a synthesis of ideas is required. The reasonable man is capable of synopsis, of viewing both or many sides of a question, of comparing various motives, of taking interest in a totality rather than in a scattered multiplicity.

You may, of course, admit that this use of the word reason is familiar; and still you may say that James's contention is nevertheless sound. For, as you may declare, the real issue is not regarding the meanings that chance to be linked with the word reason, but regarding the relative impotence of that process which James chose to call by this name. As a fact, so you may assert, there exists the familiar process of forming abstract concep-

tions; and there also exists the process of drawing
conclusions through an analysis of what is already
contained in the meaning of the assumed premises.
Whether or no one calls these two processes, in
their usual combination, by the name reasoning,
James is right in saying that abstractions, and that
such sorts of purely analytic abstract reasoning as
he has in mind, are incapable of giving us religious
insight. And both James and the others who oppose reason to concrete experience are right in asserting that you get no novel insight whatever
through mere abstractions, or through mere analysis, but are dependent for your advances in knowledge upon experience. Therefore, as you may continue, the issue which James and other empiricists
raise must not be evaded by any appeal to vaguer
uses of the word reason, whether common-sense
or the Supreme Court chances to authorise such
special forms of expression.

I fully agree to the importance of this comment
and of the issue as thus stated. I am ready to consider the issue. But I also insist upon estimating
the whole use of reason in its proper context. James,
in common with countless other partisans of intuition in religious matters, is fond of insisting that all
our nobler intuitions and all our deeper faiths are,
in their foundations, inwardly compelling, but inarticulate, and that we degrade them rather than
help them when we define their meaning in abstract
terms or employ processes of explicit demonstra-

tion in their defence. James, in common with many
empiricists, also opposes experience in general to all
processes of reasoning, and asserts that the latter
never teach us anything novel. The issue, fairly
viewed, is therefore not a perfectly simple one. It
involves the question whether the two modes of
getting knowledge between which we are asked to
choose are the only modes actually in use. Intuition, and experience in general, are by James and
by others sharply contrasted with certain processes
of abstraction and of analysis. It is then pointed
out that since these latter processes, taken by themselves, never give us any essentially novel insights,
you must on the whole cease to use your powers of
abstraction and of analysis, except for the mere
purpose of record or of teaching, or of some other
such technical end—computation, analysis of hypotheses, and the like. You must, at least in religious matters, depend upon the uprushes from
your subconscious self or upon whatever else is
persuasively inarticulate. In the ultimate decisions
of life, inarticulate intuition, mere faith, and that
alone, can save you. Hereupon the perfectly fair
question arises whether the alternatives are thus
exhaustively stated. Must one choose between inarticulate faith and barren abstractions? Must
one face the alternative: Either intuition without
reasoning, or else relatively fruitless analysis with-
ous intuition? Perhaps there is a third possibility.
Perhaps one may use one's process of abstraction

as a sort of preparation for certain articulate and
noble intuitions that cannot be approached, by our
human sort of consciousness, through any other way.
Perhaps analysis is not the whole process which determines demonstrations. Perhaps synthesis—the
viewing of many facts or principles or relations in
some sort of unity and wholeness—perhaps a synoptic
survey of various articulate truths, can lead us to
novel insights. In that case inarticulate intuitions
and barren abstractions are not the only instruments
between which we must choose. For in that case
there will be another sort of aid, a more explicit sort
of intuition, a more considerate view of our life and
its meaning, which we may adopt, and which may
lead us to novel results. And these results may be
not only articulate but saving.

Or, to state the issue more generally: In seeking
for any sort of novel truth, have we only the choice
between the experience of the data of sense or of
feeling on the one hand and the analysis of abstract
ideas and assertions upon the other? May there not
be another source of knowledge? May not this
source consist in the synthetic view of many facts in
their unity—in the grasping of a complex of relations in their total significance? And may not just
this be a source of insight which is employed in many
of the processes ordinarily known as reasoning processes? May not the formation of abstract ideas,
when wisely used, be merely a means of helping us
toward an easier view of larger unities of fact than

our present sort of human consciousness could grasp except for this auxiliary device? May not analysis be merely an aspect, a part of our live thinking? May not all genuine demonstration involve synthesis as well as analysis, the making of new constructions as well as the dissection of old assertions? If so, then the issue as presented by James and his allies is not rightly stated, because an essential part of its context is neglected. Abstract conceptions are, in fact, in the live and serious work of thought, a mere preparation for intuitions and experiences that lie on higher levels than those which, apart from abstract conceptions, we men can reach. Reasoning processes are fruitful because they involve sorts of experience, forms of intuition, that you cannot reach without them. In brief, reason and experience are not opposed. There is an opposition between inarticulate intuition and articulate insight. There is also an opposition between relatively blind experience of any sort and relatively rational experience. And, in view of such oppositions, it will be perfectly fair to define reason as the power to get articulate insight—insight into wholes rather than fragments. It will also be fair to define the reasoning process as the process of getting connected experience on a large scale.

Whoever views the matter thus will indeed not be forced to be a one-sided partisan of the reasoning process as thus defined. He will, first, fully admit that the formation of abstract ideas is but a means

to an end, and that this end is the enlargement of
the range of our view of the connections of our experience.   He will secondly admit that, as soon as
the process of forming abstract ideas is pursued as
an end in itself, pedantry and formalism result,
whether the topic be one of religion, or of science,
or of the world's daily work.   He will further agree
with James, and with the empiricists generally, that
merely analytic reasoning, if such were, in its isolation, a possible thing, would be indeed "barren intellectualism."   And finally, if he is wise, he will go
still further.   He will not despise instinct, and feeling, and the movings of faith, and the inarticulate
intuitions.   For he will know that all these things
are human, are indispensable, and are the basis upon
which the genuine work of the reason, the wider
view of life, must be carried toward its fulfilment.
For whoever is to comprehend the unities of life
must first live.   Whoever is to be best able to survey the landscape from the mountain top must first
have wandered in its paths and its byways, and must
have grown familiar with its valleys and its recesses.
Whoever is to get the mature insight must first have
become a little child.

But whoever, remembering the New Testament
word about becoming as a little child, one-sidedly
defends the inarticulate intuitions, as the only
source of religious insight, should remember also
the word of St. Paul: "When I was a child, I spake
as a child, I thought as a child, I understood as a

child; but when I became a man I put away childish things."

It is the business of reason not to make naught
of the indispensable intuitions of the childlike and of
the faithful, but to work toward the insight such
that, if we possessed it, we should "know even as
we are known." That which is weak in this world
may indeed confound many who are called wise;
but there is no objection to its becoming also truly
wise itself. For then it would all the better know
why it had been able to confound false wisdom.

III

All such considerations will seem to many of you
hopelessly general. You will have missed, thus far
in my account, concrete instances to illustrate how
what I have now called the reason actually works,
how it is related to experience, how it helps us toward the broader view of things, how it makes the
connections of life more obvious, how it raises our
intuitions to higher levels. And unfortunately,
since I have no time to discourse to you upon the
science called Logic—the science part of whose
proper duty it is to define the nature and the office
of what I have now called the reason—I must indeed fail, in this brief summary, to give you any
adequate account of what can be accomplished
through the appeal to this source of insight. All
that I shall try to do, on this occasion, is to mention

to you a very few instances, some of them relatively trivial, wherein, through reasoning processes, we actually get these larger intuitions on higher levels, these higher modes of grasping the unity of things. Having thus very imperfectly exemplified what I mean by the synthetic processes of reasoning, I shall be ready barely to suggest to you, as I close, how the reason can be, and is, a source of religious insight.

In some recent logical discussions, and in particular in my colleague Professor Hibben's text-book of logic, there has been used an example, trivial in itself, but in its own way typical—an example which is meant to show how there exists a mental process which is surely worthy of the name reasoning, and which is, nevertheless, no mere process of forming abstract ideas and no mere analysis of the meaning of assumed premises, although, of course, both abstraction and analysis have their subordinate places in this process. The reasoning involved in this example is of the very simplest sort. It is expressed in an old story which many of you will have heard.

According to this story, an aged ecclesiastic, garrulous and reminiscent, was once, in a social company, commenting upon the experiences that had come to him in his long and devoted life. Fully meaning to keep sacred the secrets of the confessional, the old man was nevertheless led to say: "Ah—it is strange, and sometimes terrible, what, in my profession, one may have to face and consider.

You must know, my friends, my very first penitent was—a murderer! I was appalled." The old priest had hardly spoken when the company was joined by an aged and prominent nobleman of the region, whom all present greeted with great respect. Saluting his priestly friend with no little reverence, the nobleman turned to the company and said, with calm unconsciousness: "You must know, my friends, in my youth I was the very first person whom my honored friend here ever confessed."

Now observe. The priest had not said who the murderer was. The nobleman in his contribution to the conversation had not confessed to the company the murder. He had not mentioned it in any way. And the priest had scrupulously avoided mentioning him. But all present drew at once the reasonable conclusion that, granting the correctness of the two assertions, the nobleman was a murderer. We, of course, must all agree in this conclusion. Now is this conclusion the result of a mere analysis of either of the two assertions made? And does the conclusion merely result from our power to form abstract ideas? Plainly, the conclusion is due to the power of all present to make a synthesis, or, as one sometimes says, to put two and two together. Plainly, whatever abstract ideas are here used, it is not these which constitute the main work of a reasonable being who views the situation in which the nobleman is placed by the whole sense of the conversation. Reason here discovers a novel fact which neither the priest nor the nobleman had stated. This discovery is as much an experience as if it were the observation of an actual killing of one man by another. Only it is the discovery of the relations involved in a synthesis of meanings. This discovery is at once empirical (yes, in the broader sense of the word intuitive), and it is a discovery of a necessary connection. It is not due to mere analysis. It is not a bit of barren intellectualism. It is not an unpractical comment. It is a discovery that might wreck the nobleman's reputation, and that might more or less indirectly lead to his ultimate conviction upon a capital charge. Now, that is an example, trivial enough if viewed as a mere anecdote, but a typical example, of the synthetic and constructive use of reason as a source of insight.

Let me turn to another also at first sight seemingly trivial case. An English logician, De Morgan, long ago called attention to a form of reasoning which, up to his time, the logicians had unduly neglected. If you assume that "a horse is an animal," you can reasonably conclude that "the owner of a horse is the owner of an animal"; that "whoever loves a horse loves an animal," and so on indefinitely. In brief, as you at once see, from the one assertion, "A horse is an animal," there rationally follow a limitless number of possible inferences of the form: "Whatever is in any relation R to a horse is in that same relation R to an animal." Now you may indeed at first, as I just said,

imagine such reasonings to be comparatively trivial.
Whether they prove to be so, however, depends
wholly upon the objects in question, upon our own
interests in these objects, and upon circumstances.
They might be vastly important. From the assertion, "Mr. Taft is President of the United States,"
there follows, by this sort of reasoning, the assertion,
"Whoever is a personal friend of Mr. Taft is a personal friend of the President of the United States."
And such a conclusion some people might be very
glad to have you draw. So, too, whoever is a mem-
ber of Mr. Taft's family, or household, or club, or of
the university whose degrees he holds, or whoever
is a fellow-townsman, or fellow-countryman, or partisan, or opponent, or enemy of Mr. Taft, whoever
agrees with what he says in his speeches, whoever
plays golf with him, or whoever hopes or fears for
his re-election, stands in just that relation, whatever it may be, to the President of the United States.
And how important such rational inferences might
appear for the comprehension of somebody's actual
situation and prospects and acts depends upon the
persons and the interests that may be in question.
To some people just such inferences, at one moment
or another, will not seem trivial, will be worth making, and will be anything but feats of barren intellectualism. That they are easy inferences to make is
beside the mark. I have no time to ask you here
to study with me the harder inferences upon topics
that do not concern our main purpose. What I

need, however, is to illustrate to you that such reasoning processes go beyond mere analysis, and do involve a rational and articulate intuition of a novel aspect of experience. For I defy you to find by any mere analysis of the assertion, "Mr. Taft is President," the innumerable assertions about friends, about family, about speeches, and policies, and so on, which as a fact rationally follow, in the indicated way, from that first assertion. You find these new results by taking a broader view of the unity of experience. What, then, I need to have you see is that the reason which, even in its lightest deeds, can accomplish such syntheses, and which can lead to such ordered intuitions, and can be the endless source of such novelties, is not merely the reason of whose powers as a source of insight James gives so discouraging a picture.

Having thus barely illustrated the thesis that reason can be both productive of new insight and constructively synthetic in its grasp of wider ranges of experience than we could observe without it, let me add that, in the exact sciences, and in particular in mathematics, the reasoning process, using just such forms of synthesis as I have now illustrated, is constantly leading investigators to the most varied and novel discoveries. These discoveries are not due to mere analysis. They are reports of facts and the results of synthetic construction. As Mr. Charles Peirce loves to point out, the new discoveries made in mathematics, and by purely rational processes, are so numerous that for each year a volume of many hundreds of closely printed pages is needed to give, with strictly technical brevity, even the barest outline of the contents of the papers containing the novel results of that one year's researches.   In their union with other sciences, the mathematical researches constantly lead to still vaster ranges of novel discovery. Reason, then, is not merely barren, is not mainly concerned with unproductive analysis, but does enrich our survey of experience, of its unity and of its meaning.

Perhaps some of you may still object that, if I define reason in the terms suggested by these instances, there seems to be danger of making the word "reason" mean simply the same as the word "insight."   For insight, as I defined it in my opening lecture, means a coherent view of many facts in some sort of unity.   And in this case, as you may now say, why use two words at all?   I reply that, in fact, all true insight is, to my mind, rational insight, upon one or another level of the development of our power to become rational beings.   But you will remember that insight, as I defined it, also means knowledge which is intimate and manifold, as well as knowledge which views facts and relations in their unity.   The words intuition and experience are often used to lay stress upon that aspect of our insight which either makes it intimate or else brings it into touch with many and various facts.   And such usage is convenient.   The word reason, as I have just exemplified its more synthetic meaning, calls our attention precisely to that aspect of our better insight which is involved in our power to grasp many facts in their *unity*, to see the coherence, the inter-relationship, the totality of a set of experiences. Now when insight reaches higher levels, these various aspects of our knowledge are never sundered. But as we grow toward higher insight, we know in part and prophesy in part and are child-like in so far as that which is perfect has not yet come.

In these, our imperfect stages of growth, sometimes our knowledge possesses intimacy, but still has to remain content, for the moment, with a more inarticulate grasp of deeper meanings. In such cases James's sort of intuition, or what is often called blind faith, is mainly in question. And this is indeed a stage on the way to insight. We feel unities but do not see them. Sometimes, however, as in much of our ordinary experience, the state of our minds is different; our knowledge revels in, or else contends with, the endless variety and multiplicity of the facts of life, and lacks a grasp of their unity. In that case our insight is often called "merely empirical." We have experience; and so far our knowledge prospers. But we neither feel vaguely nor see clearly the total sense of things. And in such cases our sight is too busy to give us time for higher insight. As the Germans say, we do not see the wood because of the trees.

In a third stage of partial insight we may stand

where, for instance, the masters of the exact sciences
stand. We then grasp, with clearness, larger unities of controllable experience. We create objects,
as the mathematicians create, in an ideal world of
our own contemplation; and we then come to see
that these ideal creations of ours do, indeed, reveal
the eternal truth regarding a world of seemingly impersonal or superpersonal reality. We learn of this
reality through the coherent synthesis of our ideal
constructions. Our intuition is in this case at once
empirical, articulate, and such as to survey the
broad landscape of the genuine relations of things.
But alas! in most such cases our objects, although
they are indeed presented to our rational intuition,
are often abstract enough in their seeming. They
are objects such as numbers, and series, and ordered
arrays of highly ideal entities. In such cases the
reason does its typical work; but often the objects
of our insight fail to meet the more intense needs of
life.

Thus, then, inarticulate intuitions, ordinary or
sometimes more scientific observations of the details
of life, and mathematical reasonings concerning the
unity and the connections of highly ideal objects
such as numbers, come to stand in our experience as
more or less sharply sundered grades of imperfect
insight. Thus we naturally come to view the typical achievements of our reason as a thing apart,
and the rational or exact sciences as remote both
from the intuitive faith of the little ones and from

the wealthy experience of the men of common-sense and of the men of natural science. As a fact, all these stages of insight are hints of what the Supreme Court meant when it appealed to the "rule of reason." True insight, if fulfilled, would be empirical, for it would face facts; intuitive, for it would survey them and grasp them, and be intimate with them; rational, for it would view them in their unity.

IV

Our lengthy effort to define the work and the place of the reason has brought us to the threshold of an appreciation of its relation to the religious insight which we are seeking.

In looking for salvation, we discover that our task is defined for us by those aspects of individual and social experience upon which our two previous lectures have dwelt. We have learned from the study of these two sorts of experience that, whatever else we need for our salvation, one of our needs is to come into touch with a life that in its unity, in its meaning, in its perfection, is vastly superior to our present human type of life. And so the question has presented itself: Have we any evidence that such a superhuman type of life is a real fact in the world? The mystics, and many of the faithful, answer this question by saying: "Yes. We have such evidence. It is the assurance that we get through intuition, through feeling, through the light revealed to us in certain moments when thought ceases, and the proud intellect is dumb, and when the divine speaks quite directly to the passive and humbled soul." Now when we calmly consider the evidence of such moments of inarticulate conviction, they strongly impress upon us what we have called the religious paradox. Faith, and the passive and mysterious intuitions of the devout, seem to depend on first admitting that we are naturally blind and helpless and ignorant, and worthless to know, of ourselves, any saving truth; and upon nevertheless insisting that we are quite capable of one very lofty type of knowledge—that we are capable, namely, of knowing God's voice when we hear it, of distinguishing a divine revelation from all other reports, of being sure, despite all our worthless ignorance, that the divine higher life which seems to speak to us in our moments of intuition is what it declares itself to be. If, then, there is a pride of intellect, does there not seem to be an equal pride of faith, an equal pretentiousness involved in undertaking to judge that certain of our least articulate intuitions are infallible?

Surely here is a genuine problem, and it is a problem for the reason. We know that men differ in faith. We know that one man's intuition regarding the way of salvation may seem to another man to be a mere delusion, a deceitful dream. We know, from the reports of religious experience, that at times even the saints of greatest renown have doubted whether some of their most persuasive visions of the

divine were not, after all, due to the cunning deceit
of an enemy of souls whom they more or less super-
stitiously feared.   We know that to common-sense,
despite its interest in salvation, the reports of the
mystics and of the faithful have often appeared to
be but the tale of private and vain imaginings.   It
is fair to ask what are the criteria whereby the true
spiritual gifts, the genuine revelations, are to be
distinguished.   And this, I insist, is a question for
the reason, for that aspect of our nature which has
to do with forming estimates of wholes rather than
of fragments—estimates of life in its entirety rather
than of this or that feeling or moment of ecstasy in
its isolation.

If, hereupon, without for the moment attempting
to discuss how others, as, for instance, James himself,
deal with the problem of the reasonable estimate of
the value of our religious intuitions, I sketch for you
my own opinion as to how reason does throw light
upon the religious paradox, I must again emphasise
a matter that I mentioned in my opening lecture and
that is much neglected.   Religious faith does, indeed,
involve a seemingly paradoxical attempt to transcend
the admitted ignorance of the needy human being,
to admit that of himself this being knows almost
nothing about the way of salvation, and nevertheless to insist that he is able to recognise his Deliverer's
voice as the voice of a real master of life when he
hears that voice, or—apart from metaphor—that he
is able to be sure what revelation of a divine life, not

his own, is the true one when he happens to get it. But religion is not alone in this paradoxical pride of humility. Science and common-sense alike involve a similar admission of the depths of our human fallibility and ignorance, on the one hand, and an analogous assurance that, despite this our fragmentariness of experience, despite our liability to be deceived, we nevertheless can recognise truth when experience once has not wholly verified it, but has sufficiently helped us to get it. For, as individuals, we are constantly confident beyond what our present experience, taken by itself, clearly reveals to us. We, for instance, trust our individual memory in the single case, while admitting its pervasive fallibility in general. We persistently view ourselves as in reasonably close touch with the general and common results of human experience, even at the moment when we have to admit how little we know about the mind or the experience of any one fellow-man, even our nearest friend. We say that some of our opinions, for instance, are warranted by the common-sense of mankind. That is, we pretend once for all to know a good deal about what the common experience of mankind is. And yet, if we look closer, we see that we do not directly see or experience the genuine inner life of any one of mankind except the private self which each one of us regards as his own, while, if we still further consider the matter, we can readily observe how little each one of us really knows even about himself. When we appeal then to what we call common-sense, we pretend to know what it is that, as we say, the mind of mankind finds to be true. But if we are asked to estimate the real state of mind of any individual man, how mysterious that state is! In brief, the paradox of feeling confidence in our own judgment, even while regarding all human opinion as profoundly fallible, is not merely a religious paradox, but also pervades our whole social and personal and even our scientific types of opinion. Not to have what is called a reasonable confidence in our own individual opinions is the mark of a weakling. But usually, if our personal opinions relate to important matters, they bring us into more or less serious conflict with at least some of the opinions of other men. Conflict is one mark that your opinions are worth having. When the conflict arises, we are usually led to consider how fallible other men are. They are fallible, we say, because they are human. How little any poor man knows! Yes, but if this principle holds true, how doubtful are my own opinions! Yet if I fill my mind with that reflection, to the exclusion of all other reasonable considerations, I condemn myself not to mere fallibility, but to certain failure.

The paradox is universal. It pervades all forms and activities of human inquiry. That is the first synthetic observation of the reason, when it surveys the field of human opinion. Everywhere we live by undertaking to transcend in opinion what the evidence before us, at any one moment, directly and infallibly warrants. But is it rational to do this? And if so, *why* is it rational?

The answer is that while there is much irrational presumption and overconfidence in our human world, there is also a perfectly rational principle which warrants certain forms and methods of thus transcending in our opinions the immediately presented evidence of the moment when we judge. This principle is as universal as it is generally neglected. Rightly understood, it simply transforms for you your whole view of the real universe in which you live.

An opinion of yours may be true or false. But when you form an opinion, what are you trying to do? You are trying to anticipate, in some fashion, what a wider view, a larger experience of your present situation, a fuller insight into your present ideas, and into what they mean, would show you, if you now had that wider view and larger experience. Such an effort to anticipate what the wider view would even now show, if you were possessed of that view, involves both what are usually called theoretical interests and what pragmatists, such as James himself, have often characterised as practical interests. One can express the matter by saying, that you are trying, through your opinions, to predict what a larger insight, if it were present to you, would show or would find, that is, would experience. You can also say that you are trying to define what

a fuller apprehension and a fairer estimate of your
present purposes, and intentions, and interests, and
deeds, and of their outcome, and of their place
in life, would bring before your vision. In brief
(whether you lay more stress upon deeds and their
outcome, or upon experiences and their contents),
any expression of opinion, made at any time, is an
appeal of the self of the moment to the verdict, to
the estimate, to the experience of a larger and better
informed insight, in the light of which the self of the
moment proposes to be judged. The special criteria
by which your momentary opinion is tested, at the
time when you form that opinion, vary endlessly
with your mood and your training and your feelings,
and with the topics and tasks in which you happen
to be interested. But the universal form in which
any opinion comes to your consciousness, and gets
its definition for your own mind, is this form of an
appeal to an insight that is superior in grasp, in
unity, in coherence, in reasonableness to your momentary insight.

Now you can indeed say: "When I form and express an opinion, I appeal from my present experiences to some wider insight that I view *as if it were*
possible. My opinion asserts that *if I were* permitted to see what I just now do not directly experience, I should find the facts to be so and so."
But no such account of the matter is quite complete.
Everything that you regard as possible has to be
conceived as somehow based upon what you regard

as actual. And so, in fact, your opinions are always
appeals to some form of wider or larger or deeper or
richer insight that, in the act of appealing to it, you
regard as a present or as a past or as a future reality
—in brief, as a live and perfectly concrete insight to
whose verdict you appeal. Philosophers often express this by saying that all opinions are nothing
but efforts to formulate the real contents of experience. This view I accept.

So then, as I insist, whatever your opinions, your
expression of them is an appeal to some wider insight that you regard as real, and that you view as
a live insight which comprehends your ideas, and
which sees how they are related to genuine experience. This, I affirm, is the universal form which all
opinion takes. A true opinion is true, because in
fact it expresses what the wider insight confirms.
A false opinion is false, because it is refuted by the
light of this same wider view. Apart from such a
confirmation or refutation in the light of such a
larger view, the very concepts of truth and error, as
applied to opinions which are not wholly confirmed
or set aside by the instantaneous evidence of the
moment when the opinions are formed or uttered,
have no meaning. True is the judgment that is
confirmed by the larger view to which it appeals.
False is the assertion that is not thus confirmed.
*Upon such a conception the very ideas of truth and
error depend. Without such a conception truth and
error have no sense.* If such a conception is not it-

self a true view of our situation, that is, if there is
no wider insight, our opinions have neither truth nor
error, and are all of them alike merely meaningless.
When you are ignorant, you are ignorant of what
the wider view makes clear to its own insight. If
you blunder or are deluded, your blunder is due
to a defective apprehension which the wider view
confirms. And thus, whether you are ignorant or
blundering, wise or foolish, whether the truth or the
falsity of your present opinion is supposed to be
actual, one actuality is equally and rationally presupposed, as the actuality to which all your opinions
refer, and in the light of which they possess sense.
*This is the actuality of some wider insight with refer-
ence to which your own opinion gets its truth or its
falsity.*

To this wider insight, to this always presupposed
vision of experience as it is, of the facts as they are,
you are always appealing. Your every act of assertion displays the genuineness of the appeal and exemplifies the absolute rational necessity of asserting
that the appeal is made to an insight that is itself
real.

Frequently you do, indeed, call this insight merely
the common-sense of mankind. But, strange to say,
this common-sense of mankind is always and inevitably conceived by you in terms that distinguish
it from the fleeting momentary views of any or of
all merely individual men. Men—if I may judge
them by my own case, and by what I hear other

men confess—men, when taken merely as individuals, always live from moment to moment in a flickering way, normally confident, indeed, but clearly seeing at any one instant very little at a time. They are narrow in the span of the more direct insight. They grasp data bit by bit, and comprehend, in their instantaneous flashes of insight, only little scraps and tiny bundles of ideas. I who now speak to you cannot hold clearly and momentarily before my mind at once even all of the meaning that I try to express in two or three of my successive sentences. I live looking before and after, and pining for what is not, and grasping after unity; and I find each moment crumbling as it flies; and each thought and each sentence of my discourse drops into momentary forgetfulness so soon as I have carefully built up its passing structure. In our life all thus flows. We fly from one flash of insight to another.

But nevertheless our opinions, so we say, reflect sometimes the common-sense of mankind. They conform to the verdict of humanity. But who amongst us ever goes beyond thus confidently holding that he reflects the common-sense of mankind? Who amongst us personally and individually experiences, at any moment, the confirmation said to be given by the verdict of humanity? The verdict of humanity? What man ever finds immediately presented to his own personal insight that totality of data upon which this verdict is said to depend?

The common-sense of mankind?   What mortal man
is there who ever finds incorporated in his flickering,
fleeting, crumbling, narrow moments of personal experience the calm and secure insight which this
common-sense of mankind, or of enlightened mankind, is said to possess?

No, the common-sense of mankind is, for us all, a
sort of super-individual insight, to which we appeal
without ourselves fully possessing it.   This "*common*"-sense of mankind is just the sense *which no
man of us all ever individually possesses.*   For us all
it is, indeed, something superhuman.   We spend part
of our busy little lives in somewhat pretentiously
undertaking to report its dicta.   But it is simply one
of the countless forms in which we conceive the
wider insight to be incorporated.   *The true rational
warrant for this confidence of ours lies in the fact that
whatever else is real, some form of such a wider insight,
some essentially super-individual and superhuman insight is real.*   For unless it is real our opinions, including any opinion that we may have that doubts
or questions or denies its reality, are all equally
meaningless.   Thus even when we appeal to common-sense we really appeal to a genuine but superhuman insight.

Let us not here spend time, however, upon analysing this or that special form in which we are accustomed, for one special purpose or another, to conceive
the wider insight.   What is clear is that we constantly, and in every opinion, in every confession of

ignorance appeal to such an insight.   That such an
insight is real, must be presupposed even in order to
assert that our present opinions are errors.   What
interests us most at this point is, however, this, that
whatever else the whole real universe is, the real
universe exists only in case it is the object, and the
very being, of such an insight, of such an inclusive
experience, of such a view of what is.   For, when
you hold any opinions whatever about the real
world, or about any of its contents, characters, or
values, your opinions are either true or false, and
are true or false by virtue of their actual conformity
to the live insight which experiences what makes
them true or false, and which therefore *ipso facto*
experiences what the real world is.   If there is *no*
such world-possessing insight, then, once more, your
opinions about the world are neither true nor false.
Or, otherwise stated, if there is no such inclusive
insight there is no world.   To the real world, then,
this insight which comprehends the world, and which
knows whatever is true to be true, and whatever is
false about the world to be false—to the real world
this insight, I say, belongs.   And the whole world
belongs to it and is its object and essence.   Whatever is real is real for that insight, and is in its experience, and exists as its possession, and as its well-
known and well-comprehended content, and as its
image and expression and meaning.

All this I say, as you may note, not because I
hold in high esteem any of our private human opin-

ions, but only because, *except in the light of such an all-seeing comprehension of facts as they are, our individual opinions about the world cannot even be false.* For opinion, in all its fleeting blindness and in its human chaos of caprices, is ceaselessly an appeal to the judge, to the seer, to the standard experience, to the knower of facts as they are, to the wider view, to the decisive insight. And opinions about reality in its wholeness, about the world, about the all, are appeals to the all-judging insight, to the all-seeing view, to the knowledge and experience that grasps the totality of facts, to the widest outlook, to the deepest insight, to the absolute rational decision. If this be so, then an opinion to the effect that there exists no such widest and deepest insight, and no such final view, is itself just such an appeal to the final insight, simply because it is an opinion about reality. To assert then that there is no largest view, no final insight, no experience that is absolute, is to assert that the largest view observes that there is no largest view, that the final insight sees that there is no such insight, that the ultimate experience is aware that there is no ultimate experience. And such an assertion is indeed a self-contradiction.

This, I assert, is the only rational way of stating the nature of opinion, of truth or error, and consequently of reality. This is the synthesis which reason inevitably accomplishes whenever it rightly views the nature and the implications of even our most flickering and erroneous and uncertain opin-

ions. We can err about what you will. But if we
err, we simply come short of the insight to which
we are aiming to conform, and in the light of which
our ideas get absolutely all of their meaning. In
every error, in every blunder, in all our darkness, in
all our ignorance, we are still in touch with the eternal
insight. We are always seeking to know even as we
are known.

I have sought in this sketch to vindicate the general rights of rational insight as against mere momentary or fragmentary intuition. I have also
tried to show you what synthesis of reason gives us
a genuinely religious insight.

"My first penitent," said the priest of our story,
"was a murderer." "And I," said the nobleman,
"was this priest's first penitent."

"I am ignorant of the vast and mysterious real
world"—thus says our sense of human fallibility
and weakness when we are first awakened to our
need of rational guidance. The saying is true.
The mystery is appalling. "I am ignorant of the real
world." Yes; but reason, reflecting upon the nature
and the essential meaning of opinion, of truth, of
error, and of ignorance, points out to us this thesis:
"That of which I am ignorant is that about which
I can err. But error is failure to conform my momentary opinion to the very insight which I mean
and to which I am all the while appealing. Error
is failure to conform to the inclusive insight which

overarches my errors with the heaven of its rational clearness. Error is failure to grasp the very light which shines in my darkness, even while my darkness comprehends it not. That of which I am ignorant is then essentially the object of a superhuman and divine insight."

"I am ignorant of the world. To be ignorant is to fail to grasp the object of the all-inclusive and divine insight." That is the expression of our situation. Reason easily makes the fitting synthesis when it considers the priest and the nobleman. I ask you to make the analogous synthesis regarding the world and the divine insight. This synthesis here takes form in concluding that the world is the object of an all-inclusive and divine insight, which is thus the supreme reality.

I have but sketched for you the contribution of reason to our quest. This contribution will seem to many of you too abstract and too contemplative to meet vital religious needs. In fact, what I have said will mean little to you unless you come to see how it can be translated into an adequate expression in our active life. To this task of such a further interpretation of the mission of the reason as a guide of life my next lecture shall be devoted.

IV

THE WORLD AND THE WILL

IV

THE WORLD AND THE WILL

I COULD not discuss, in my last lecture, the office of the reason as a source of religious insight without sketching for you what insight I personally regard as the most important result of the right use of reason. This sketch was of course, in my own mind, a part of an extended body of philosophical doctrine. It does not lie within the intent of these lectures to present a system of philosophy. I ought, nevertheless, to begin this lecture by saying a few words about the relation of my last discussion to certain religious and philosophical opinions of which you have all heard, and by indicating why it has seemed to me worth while to call your attention to the mere hint of a philosophy with which the last discussion closed. Having thus indicated the setting in which I want you to see the brief exposition of a general theory which I find to be indispensable for our main purpose, I shall devote the rest of this lecture to the task of connecting the insight which reason gives to us with the main purpose of our inquiry, namely, with the undertaking to know the nature and the way of salvation. Reason is of importance in so far as what it shows us enables us to direct our will and to come into closer touch with truths which are not only theoretical, but also practical.

We shall therefore discuss at some length the relation of our rational knowledge to our active life, and the relation of our rational will to the world in which we are to work out our salvation if we can.

I

The nature and the teachings of the human reason have interested philosophers from very nearly the beginning of philosophical inquiry. What I told you about the subject in our former discussion reports a decidedly modern version of a very old opinion—an opinion which has been repeatedly examined, revised, assailed, and defended. Let me say a word as to its history.

Plato held that, through our reason, we are able to rise beyond the world of sense and to hold communion with a realm of ideally significant and eternal being. What Plato really meant by his ideal realm, and in what sense the world of what Plato called the eternal realities, the forms or ideas, could be, as Plato held it to be, a divine world, in its worth and dignity, later philosophy repeatedly attempted to grasp.

The results of such philosophical thinking have deeply affected the history of religion and still influence the religious interest of all of you. One ver-

sion of that philosophical tradition whose origin is
in the thought of Plato—a late version, and also one
greatly transformed by motives of which Plato had
known in his day nothing, is the familiar version to
which, in the last lecture, I in passing alluded—the
prologue to our Fourth Gospel. You will all agree
that this prologue attempts to state a religious insight. The relation of this New Testament view of
the world of the reason to the doctrine which still
later came to be formulated by the theologians of
the Christian Church I have here not time to discuss. It is enough now to say that an opinion according to which our articulate reason, as well as the
more inarticulate intuition of faith, has some sort of
access to the world of the "Logos," and some sort
of participation in a genuine apprehension of the
divine life, has come to form part of the religion in
which you all have been trained. In so far, then,
it is surely right to say that the reason, as the philosophers have defined it, has been an actual source of
religious opinion and experience.

In modern times, and especially since Kant, philosophy has been led to see the older doctrines of the
human reason, and of its knowledge of the divine,
from various decidedly novel points of view. The
sketch of a theory of the reason as a source of insight,
which I gave, was influenced by Kant's famous
teaching about the nature and unity of human experience. Kant stated this theory as the doctrine
that all our human knowledge involves an inter-

pretation of the data of our senses in the light of
what he called the "unity of apperception." In less
technical terms, Kant's meaning is that all facts of
which a human experience can obtain knowledge
are known to us as the possible objects of an insight
which we conceive to be virtually one, as the insight of our own truly knowing Self, and as the insight without reference to which no opinion of ours
has any sense whatever. This one cognitive Self is,
according to Kant, the conceived virtual subject
or possessor of all that we view as our experience.
And this presupposed unity is the condition of all
our knowledge.

But Kant's doctrine, as he stated it, is in many
ways problematic and dissatisfying. The form of
philosophical idealism which I myself defend goes
in certain respects far beyond Kant's position.
The "one experience," in which, according to him,
we find a place for any fact which we conceive as
knowable at all, is defined by Kant as a virtual insight, not, so to speak, a live and concrete consciousness. He regards it also as purely human, as
a knowledge of appearances—not of any ultimate
realities. The form of philosophical idealism which,
at the last time, I outlined depends, however, upon
simply universalising, and rendering live and concrete, Kant's conception of the Self, of the united
experience, to which we appeal, and in the light of
which our opinions get all their sense—all their
character and value as true or as false opinions.

This one Self, this unity of experience, to which we always appeal, cannot consistently be viewed by us as merely our own individual or private self, or as merely human; and its insight cannot rationally be interpreted merely as an insight into what is apparent, that is into what is not really real. Nor can it be viewed merely as something virtual—a possible unity of experience, to which we would appeal if we could. In my opinion it must be conceived as *more* live and real and concrete and conscious and genuine than are any of our passing moments of fleeting human experience. It must be viewed as an actual and inclusive and divinely rational knowledge of all facts in their unity. And the very nature of facts, their very being as facts, must be determined by their presence as objects in the experience of this world-embracing insight. This was the philosophical theory that I sketched in my former lecture. This is my view of what reason teaches.

Now this thesis, this somewhat remote descendant of the Platonic doctrine of the function of reason, this modern version of the concept of the "Logos" as the light that "shineth in the darkness" of our ordinary human experience, this revision and transformation of the Kantian theory of knowledge, has, by virtue of the long history of the doctrine in question, and by virtue of the difficult considerations upon which, as a philosophical thesis, it rests, a highly technical character. This technical aspect of the teaching in question forbids, in these lectures, any adequate exposition, or criticism, or defence of its problems and of its merits as a basis for a system of philosophy. And you will surely not find unnatural the fact that a study of the function of the reason should indeed involve such technical and complex issues. I mention these issues only to say at once how and how far, in the present lectures, we are concerned with them.

We are seeking a way of salvation. And in these discussions we are mainly concerned with the sources of insight into what that way is. I am not attempting to work out, in your presence, a systematic philosophy. Why, then, have I introduced this mere sketch of philosophical idealism into our inevitably crowded programme? I answer: I have done so because I have wanted to illustrate the office of reason by telling you in my own way how I view the matter. The reason is, in fact, a source of religious insight to many people who do not reflect upon its deliverances as philosophers seek to reflect, and who may not agree with me in what little I have time to expound of my own philosophical opinions. My effort has been to tell in philosophical terms what such people really mean.

In such people reason very often shows itself indirectly and concretely, by its fruits, through their deeds, through their purpose, in a word, through their will. We shall ere long see how this can be and is the case. Reason is present in such lives and inspires them. A genuine relation to some

spirit of all truth, a perfectly sincere touch with an
articulate and universal insight, a translation of the
lesson and the meaning of the synthetic reason into a
definite practical postulate that life shall be and is
an essentially reasonable and therefore an essentially divine enterprise—such I find to be the essence of the religious insight of many serious minds.
Beside the earnest devotion of such people to the
business which life assigns to them, the mere theories
of a philosopher may seem shadowy enough. And
if such people comment upon what they hear of my
philosophy by saying that they do not understand
it, and doubt whether they agree with it, I am not
on that account at all disposed to complain of them,
or to assert that reason is to them no source of
religious insight. I take pleasure, however, in observing that, in my opinion, they agree with my
doctrine in the concrete, and express it in their
religious life far better than I can express it in my
technical terms, however much these people may
fail to grasp what my terms mean or to accept my
formulations. The best expression of your reason
is your life, if you live as one enlightened from above
ought to live. You are not obliged to accept a
technical formula in order to embody the spirit of
that formula in your daily work. I know many
men who are far more the servants and ministers
of the true rational insight than, in my present
human life, I shall ever succeed in becoming, and
who, nevertheless, either are impatient of every

philosophical theory, or, if philosophically trained, are opposed to me in my philosophy.

Nevertheless, I need to express, in my own way, what is the insight that is really at the heart of the lives of just such people. What I am first interested in emphasising is of course this, that, in my opinion, my interpretation of the insight of which reason is the source, actually expresses one important aspect of the spirit in which those live whom I regard as the true servants of the divine reason. But my interest in the matter does not cease here. I can, of course, express my opinions only in the terms that appeal to me. But whatever you think of my formulas, I am very anxious to have you see that, as the life of such people convincingly shows, reason has been, and is, a source of religious insight to them, and that our philosophical differences relate simply to the way in which we formulate our interpretation of the meaning of this source.

Reason has been such a source of insight. That is true as an historical fact. If you can find anything in the Platonic dialogues which appeals to you as involving an insight that has religious value, you must recognise this truth. It is a mere matter of history that Christian doctrine as it has come down to us is, in one aspect, profoundly affected by Plato's influence. The myth of the men in the cave, in the "Platonic Republic," the myth in Plato's "Phædrus," which tells about the banishment of the soul from its heavenly life and from its intercourse with the ideal world, and which interprets all our loftier human loves as a longing of the soul for its divine home land—these myths are allegories which Plato intended to illustrate his own view of what reason teaches us. These myths express in figurative speech a philosophy that actually affects to-day your own religious interests. For instance, this philosophy influences your traditional conception of God, and your ideas about the immortal life of the soul. And if the prologue of the Fourth Gospel seems to you to contain any truth, your religious ideas are again moulded by a form of ancient philosophy which dealt with the nature and with the insight of the reason. My own sketch of modern philosophy is but a reinterpretation of the very truth which that ancient doctrine attempted to portray. Historically, then, some of your religious opinions are actually due to the work of the reason. My philosophy simply tries to interpret to you this work.

And reason not only has been, but now is, such a source of insight. And this is the case whenever you try to apply the "rule of reason" to any problem of your life, and hereby gain a confidence that, by being as reasonable and fair as you can, you are learning to conform your life to the view which, as you suppose, an all-wise God takes of its meaning. My philosophy simply tries to tell you why you have a right to hold that an all-wise being is real.

I am anxious, I say, to have such facts about the

office of reason recognised, whatever you may think of my philosophy. And this is my purpose when I use my philosophy merely to illustrate the office of reason. For indispensable as individual religious experience is, in all the capriciousness of its feelings —indispensable also as social religious experience is, with all its insistence upon human love and also upon human religious convention—the synthetic use of the reason, that is, the systematic effort "to see life steadily and see it whole," is also indispensable. The recent efforts to make light of the work of reason —efforts to which, at the last lecture, I directed your attention, would tend, if taken by themselves, to result in basing religion upon an inarticulate occultism, upon a sort of psychical research that would regard whatever witch may peep and mutter, whatever mystic may be unable to tell what he means, whatever dumb cry of the soul may remain stubbornly inarticulate, as a *more* promising religious guide than is any form of serious and far-seeing devotion to the wider insight, which ought to survey life and to light our path.

Let my own appeal to philosophy, then, even if you do not agree with my formulas, stand as my protest against occultism and against the exclusive devotion to the inarticulate sources of religious insight. That I also prize the perfectly indispensable office of the more child-like intuitions, when they occupy their true place, you already know from my first two lectures. We cannot in our present life

do without these child-like intuitions. We cannot
be just to them without aiming to live beyond them
and to put away childish things.

II

If my interpretation of the reason thus gets its
worth from the fact that it attempts by a formula
simply to illustrate the view which the servants of
the divine reason actually and practically translate
into life, and express through their spirit and through
their deeds, you may hereupon object that my view
of the reason as a source of religious insight still
seems to you to be one which it is not easy to translate into life at all. What does it profit a man, you
will say, to view the whole world as the object
present to an all-embracing and divine insight?
How does such a view give a man the power to live
more reasonably than he otherwise would live? Is
a world-embracing reason that sees all things in
their unity really that master of life whom our simpler religious intuitions call upon us to seek as our
Deliverer from our natural chaos of desires? I have
just asserted that there are people who devote their
lives to the service of such a divine reason. But if
the divine reason is eternal and perfect, and if it
sees all reality as an unity, and if this is its only
function, how can any one serve it at all? The
eternal needs no help, you may insist, and apparently has no concern for us. We need, for our sal-

vation, something, or some personal deliverer, that
can teach us not merely to utter true assertions, but
to live worthy lives. How does the insight of the
reason enlighten us in this respect? What would
one do for a divine Logos, for an all-observant and
all-comprehending seer? Could one love such a
being, or devoutly commune with his perfect but
motionless wisdom? Is it true then, as I have just
maintained it to be true, that the insight of the
reason, as I have expounded it in my sketch of a
philosophy, does really inspire the earnest and devoted souls whose spirit I have attempted to express?
Whatever they may think of my philosophy, have I
been just to their practical fervour and to their ener-
getic devotion? Do they merely say: God is om-
niscient, therefore our life has its purpose defined,
and we are saved?

In brief, the insight of the reason, as I have been
stating its dicta, may seem to you, at best, to show
us a sort of heaven which, as I said, overarches our
unwisdom with its starry clearness, but which as
you may now add we can neither reach, nor use,
nor regard as a rational inspiration of our active
life. If it is real, it can observe us, as it observes
all reality. But can it save us? It can rise above
us. But can it enter into our will and give us a
plan of life? Granting the validity of the argument
sketched in our last lecture, what has the all-wise
knower of truth to do with our salvation?

These are familiar objections to such a view as

mine. James repeatedly urged them in his comment upon what he regarded as not merely the fallibility, but the futility, or, as he said, the "thinness" of the idealistic interpretation of the world of the reason. Similar objections have been urged by many of the critics of any doctrine similar to mine. Are these objections just?

III

I can answer such questions only through a certain gradual approach to their complications. I want to show you how the insight of the reason not only points out a heaven that overarches us, but also reveals an influence that can inwardly transform us. To this end I shall next illustrate, by instances taken from life, how some people actually view their own personal relations to what they take to be the divine reason. I shall thus indicate in what way such people connect this divine reason with personal needs of their own which they regard as vital. Then I shall show why this not only is so in the lives of some people, but ought to be so for all of us. As a result we shall soon find that, just as our first statement of the insight of reason, if indeed it is a true statement, transforms our view of the sense in which the world is real, so a deeper study of the relations of insight to action transforms our first cruder notion of the reason itself, of its office in life, and of the truth that it rereveals.

I begin with illustrations taken from life. A former college student of mine, some of whose papers upon his own religious experience I was not very long ago privileged to read, undertook, in one of these papers, to explain how, at the time, he viewed the place of prayer in his own life. He was a man capable, upon the one hand, of deep emotion and of rich inner life, but on the other hand highly self-critical and disposed to doubt. After a somewhat plentiful early interest in religion, the result of home training and of personal experience, he had come, as he studied more, and looked about his world more critically, to part company almost altogether with positive faiths about religious matters. His childhood beliefs had dropped away. Doubts and disbeliefs had taken their place. In opinion, when he wrote his papers for me, he was mainly disposed to a pure naturalism. The gods of the past had vanished from his life almost altogether.

"But," said he, in his account (I follow not his exact words but their general sense), "one old religious exercise I have never quite given up. That was and is prayer. A good while ago I dropped all conventional forms of prayer. I did not say my prayers in the old way. And when I prayed I no longer fancied that the course of nature or of my luck was going to be altered for my sake, or that my prayers would help me to avoid any consequences of my folly or my ignorance. I did not pray to get anybody to mix in my affairs, so as to get me things that I wanted. But this was, and is, my feeling about prayer: When things are too much for me, and I am down on my luck, and everything is dark, I go alone by myself, and I bury my head in my hands, and I think hard that God must know it all and will see how matters really are, and understands me, and in just that way alone, by understanding me, will help me. And so I try to get myself together. And that, for me, is prayer."

I cannot repeat my student's precise form of expression. I think that I express to you the spirit of what he wrote. In any case, this form of prayer is not peculiar to that man. You see in what way the thought of the divine wisdom became a practical thought for him—a thought at once rational and, as far as it went, saving. When life shattered his little human plans—well, he lifted up his eyes unto the hills. He won a sort of conscious and reasonable union with the all-seeing life. He did not ask its aid as a giver of good fortunes. He waited patiently for the light. Now I do not think that to be an expression of the whole insight of reason; but, so far as it went, that sort of prayer was an essentially religious act. And for that youth it was also a very practical act.

Let me turn to another case. Many years ago I well knew a man, much older than myself, who has long since died. A highly intelligent man, ambitious for the things of the spirit, he was also beset with some defects of health and with many worldly cares. His defects of health made him sensitive to the sort of observation that his physical weaknesses often attracted. In addition, he had enemies, and once had to endure the long-continued trial of a public attack upon his reputation—an attack from which he at length came forth triumphant, but not without long suffering. Once I heard him telling about his own religion, which was the faith of a highly independent mind. "What I most value about my thought of God," he in effect said, "is that I conceive God as the one who knows us through and through, and who estimates us not as we seem, but as we are, and who is absolutely fair in his judgment of us." My friend had no concern for future rewards and punishments. The judgment of God to which he appealed, and in which, without any vanity, he delighted, was simply the fair and true judgment, the divine knowing of us all just as we are.

Now do you not know people whose religion is of this sort? And are not all such forms of religion, as far as they go, practical? Is the recognition of an all-seeing insight, as something real, not in itself calming, sustaining, rationalising? Does it not at the very least awaken in us the ideal which I repeatedly mentioned in our last lecture, the ideal of knowing ourselves even as we are known, and of guiding our lives in the light of such a view of ourselves? Can such an ideal remain wholly a matter of theory? Is it not from its very essence an appeal to the will?

Was not my elder friend finding a guiding principle of action in a world where he was often misunderstood? Could one steadily conceive God in these terms without constantly renewing one's power to face the world with courage?

Surely you all know many people who value the divine as they define the divine, mainly because they conceive God as what they call the Great Companion. And, for many such, it is the intimately perfect insight of this companion that they seem to themselves most to value. The ways of this companion are to them mysterious. But he knows them. They repeat the word: "He knoweth the way that I take." He sees them. He is close to them. He estimates them. So they view the matter. Is not such a conception a vitally important spring of action for those who possess it?

These illustrations suggest that one ill appreciates the insight of reason, even as so imperfectly and one-sidedly sketched by me at the last lecture, who does not see that this insight has an extremely close connection with the will.

IV

Our illustrations have now prepared the way for a general review of the relations between our reason and our will. We are ready at length to ask whether any insight of reason, whether any general view of the nature and of the unity of the world or of life, could possibly be a merely theoretical insight. And if we rightly answer this question, we shall be prepared to reply to the objection that, according to the doctrine of the last lecture, the divine insight which overarches our ignorance, and which has all reality for its object, is a lifeless, or an unpractical, or a merely remote type of pure knowledge.

Our attempt to deal with this new question can best be made by taking a direct advantage of what some of you may suppose to be the most formidable of all objections to the whole argument of the last lecture. In my sketch of a philosophy of the reason, I have so far deliberately avoided mentioning what many of you will have had in mind as you have listened to me, namely, that doctrine about our knowledge, and about truth, and about our mode of access to truth, which to-day goes by the name of Pragmatism. Here we have to do, once more, with some of the favourite theses of James's later years. We have also to do with a view with which my present audience is likely to be familiar, at least so far as concerns both the name pragmatism and the best-known fundamental theses of the pragmatist. For I speak in the immediate neighbourhood of one of the most famous strongholds of the recent pragmatic movement. I can give but a comparatively small portion of our limited time to the task of explaining to you how I view those aspects of pragmatism which here concern our enterprise. Yet this summary discussion will go far, I hope, to show how

I view the relations between the reason and the will, and in how far our will also seems to me to be a source of religious insight.

That human knowledge is confined to the range furnished by human experience, and cannot be used to transcend that experience, is an opinion widely represented in all modern discussion, and especially in the most recent times. My own account of the insight which I refer to the reason depends not upon simply ignoring this general doctrine about the limitations of our human knowledge, but upon an effort to get a rational view of what it is that we mean by human experience. My result, as I have stated it, may have seemed paradoxical; and I am far from supposing that my brief sketch could remove this paradoxical seeming, or could answer all objections. My thesis is essentially this, that you cannot rationally conceive what human experience is, and means, except by regarding it as the fragment of an experience that is infinitely richer than ours, and that possesses a world-embracing unity and completeness of constitution. My argument for this thesis has been dependent on an assertion about the sense in which any opinion whatever can be either true or false, and upon a doctrine regarding that insight to which we appeal whenever we make any significant assertion.

Now this argument will seem to some of you to have been wholly set aside by that account of the nature of judgments, of assertions, and of their truth or falsity, which pragmatism has recently maintained. A new definition of truth, you will say—or, an old definition revived and revised; a new clearness also as to the ancient issues of philosophy; an equally novel recent assimilation of philosophical methods to those that have long been prominent in natural science—these things have combined, at the present moment, to render the Platonic tradition in philosophy and the laborious deductions of Kant, as well as the speculations of the post-Kantian idealists, no longer interesting. I ought, you may insist, to have taken note of this fact before presenting my now antiquated version of the idealistic doctrine of the reason. I ought to have considered fairly the pragmatist's theory of truth. I should then have seen that our human experience may safely be left and must rationally be left, to fight its own way to salvation without any aid from the idea of an universal or all-embracing or divine insight.

How does pragmatism view the very problem about the truth and error of our human opinions which has led me to such far-reaching consequences? For the first, it is the boast of pragmatists that they deal, by preference, with what they call "concrete situations," and our "concrete situation" as human beings dealing with reality is, as they maintain, something much more readily comprehensible than is the idealistic theory of a divine insight. Truth and error are characters that belong to our asser-tions for reasons which need no overarching heavenly insight to make them clear. In brief, as the pragmatists tell us, the story of the nature of truth and of error is this:

An assertion, a judgment, is always an active attitude of a man, whereby, at the moment when he makes this assertion he directs the course of his further activities. To say "My best way out of the woods lies in that direction" is, for a wanderer lost in the forest, simply to point out a rule or plan of action and to expect certain results from following out that plan. This illustration of the man in the woods is due to James. An analogous principle, according to pragmatism, holds for any assertion. To judge is to expect some concrete consequence to follow from some form of activity. An assertion has meaning only in so far as it refers to some object that can be defined in empirical terms and that can be subjected to further direct or indirect tests, whereby its relations to our own activities can become determinate. Thus, then, a judgment, an opinion, if it means anything concrete, is always an appeal to more or less accessible human experience—and is not, as I have been asserting, an appeal to an overarching higher insight. When you make any significant assertion, you appeal to whatever concrete human observations, experiments, or other findings of data, actual or possible, can furnish the test that the opinion calls for. If I assert: "It will rain to-morrow," the assertion is to be verified or refuted by the experience of men just as they live, from moment to moment.

It remains to define, a little more precisely, wherein consists this empirical verification or refutation for which a human opinion calls. An opinion is a definite one, as has just been said, because it guides the will of the person who holds the opinion to some definite course of action. An opinion then, if sincere and significant, has *consequences*, leads to deeds, modifies conduct, and is thus the source of the experiences which one gets as a result of holding that opinion and of acting upon it. In brief, an opinion has what the pragmatists love to call its "*workings.*" Now when the workings of a given opinion, the empirical results to which, through our actions, it leads, agree with the expectations of the one who holds the opinion, the opinion is to be called true. Or, in the now well-known phrase, "An idea (or opinion) is true if it works." To use the repeated example of Professor Moore, an opinion that a certain toothache is due to a condition present in a given tooth is true, when an operation performed upon that tooth, and performed as a consequence of that opinion, and with the expectation of curing the toothache works as expected. For the operation is itself one of the workings of the opinion in question.

To assert an opinion, then, is not to appeal to an essentially superior insight, but is to appeal to the workings that follow from this opinion when you act upon it in concrete life. No other sort of truth is knowable.

A consequence of these views, often insisted upon by pragmatists, is that truth is relative to the various "concrete situations" which arise; so that absolute or final truth is indefinable by us mortals. Hence an opinion may be true for a given purpose, or in one situation (because in that situation its workings prove to be as expected), although it is relatively false when applied to some other situation, or to some wider range of experience. Absolute truth is as unobservable by us in our experience as is absolute position or absolute motion in the physical world. Every truth is definable with reference to somebody's intentions, actions, and successes or failures. These things change from person to person, from time to time, from plan to plan. What is true from the point of view of my plans need not be so from your point of view. The workings of an opinion vary in their significance with the expectations of those concerned. Truth absolute is at best a mere ideal, which for us throws no light upon the nature of the real world.

Thus, at a stroke, pragmatism, as understood by its chief representatives at the present time, is supposed to make naught of the subtle, and, as the pragmatists say, airy and fantastic considerations upon which my sketch of a philosophical idealism at the last lecture depended. Truth, they insist, is a perfectly human and for us mortals not in the least a supernatural affair. We test it as we can, by following the experienced workings to which our ideas lead. If these workings are what we meant them to be, our opinions are just in so far proven true. If no human and empirical tests of the workings of an opinion are accessible to us, the opinion remains in so far meaningless. If concrete tests lead to workings that disappoint our human expectations, our opinions are in so far false. Moreover (and upon this all the pragmatists lay great stress), truth is for us a temporal affair. It changes, it flows, it grows, it decays. It can be made eternal only by tying ourselves, for a given purpose, to abstract ideas which we arbitrarily require to remain, like mathematical definitions, unchanged. Even such ideas have no sense apart from the uses to which they can be put. Concrete truth grows or diminishes as our successes in controlling our experience, through acting upon our beliefs, wax or wane. Truth is subject to all the processes of the evolution of our concrete lives. The eternal is nothing that can be for us a live presence. What we deal with is, like ourselves, fluent, subject to growth and decay, dynamic, and never static. The pragmatist recoils with a certain mixture of horror and amusement from the conception of an all-inclusive divine insight. That, he says, would be something static. Its world of absolute reality would be a "block universe" and itself merely an aspect of a part, or perhaps the whole, of just this block. Its supposed truth would be static like itself, and therefore dead.

But does pragmatism forbid us to have religious insight? No; James, in ways which you have repeatedly heard me mention, insists that pragmatism leaves open ample room for what he thinks to be the best sort of religion, namely, for a religion suited to what he calls the "dramatic temper" of mind. Truth, so far as we men can attain to it, has indeed to be human enough. But nothing forbids us to entertain the belief that there are superhuman and supernatural realities, forms of being, living and spiritual personalities, or superpersonalities, as various and lofty as you please, provided only that they be such as to make whatever evidence of their being is accessible to us capable of definition in a human and empirical way. The truth, namely, of our belief about such beings, has to be tested by us in terms of our own concrete religious experience. Such beliefs, like others, must "work" in order to be true. That is, these beliefs, however they arise, must lead to conduct; and the results of this conduct must tend to our religious comfort, to our unity of feeling, to our peace, or power, or saintliness, or other form of spiritual perfection. The fruits of the spirit are the empirical tests of a religious doctrine; and, apart from those uprushes of faith from the subconscious whereof we have spoken in previous lectures, there are for James no other tests of the truth of religious convictions than these. The truth of religion consists in its successful "workings."

Hence, however, religion depends upon an ever-

renewed testing of its opinions through a carrying
of them out in life. Insight would be barren were
it not quickened and applied through our will. To
James, as we already know, reason, as such, seems
to be of little use in religion. But action, resolute
living, testing of your faith through your works and
through its own workings, this is religion—an endlessly restless and dramatic process, never an union
with any absolute attainment of the goal.

V

Now in what way can I hope, you may ask, to
answer these impressive and to many recent writers decisive considerations of the pragmatists? My
answer, like my foregoing statement of my own
form of idealism, depends upon extremely simple
considerations. Their interest for our discussion
lies in the fact that they have to do with the relation between reason and action, and between the real
world and the human will. As a fact, the will as
well as the reason is a source of religious insight.
No truth is a saving truth—yes, no truth is a truth
at all unless it guides and directs life. Therein I
heartily agree with current pragmatism and with
James himself. On the other hand, the will is a
collection of restless caprices unless it is unified by
a rational ideal. And no truth can have any workings at all, without even thereby showing itself to
be, just in so far as it actually works, an eternal

truth. And, furthermore, what I have asserted about
the insight which the reason gives us is so far from
being opposed to the pragmatist's facts, that every
rational consideration of the type of truth which
they define leads us back to the consideration of
absolute truth and to the assertion of an all-inclusive
insight. Only, when we view this all-inclusive insight from the point of view which the pragmatists
now emphasise (and which I myself have emphasised from a period long antedating the recent pragmatist movement), such a fair estimate of the insight
of reason transforms our first and superficial opinion of its nature and of its meaning. It becomes
the insight of a rational will, whose expression is the
world, and whose life is that in which we too live
and move and have our being.

Let me briefly dwell on each of the considerations
which I here have in mind. To me, as a philosophical student, they are not new; for, as I repeat, I insisted upon them years ago, before the modern
pragmatistic controversy began.

First, then, there are certain respects in which I
fully agree with recent pragmatism. I agree that
every opinion expresses an attitude of the will, a
preparedness for action, a determination to guide a
plan of action in accordance with an idea. Whoever
asserts anything about the way out of the woods, or
about the cause and possible cure of a toothache,
defines a course of action in accordance with some
purpose, and amongst other things predicts the pos-

sible outcome of that course of action. The outcome that he predicts is defined in terms of experience, and, so far as that is possible, in terms of
human experience. And now this is true, not only
of assertions or opinions about toothaches. It is
true also of assertions about all objects in heaven
or earth. There is no such thing as a purely in-
tellectual form of assertion which has no element of
action about it. An opinion is a deed. It is a deed
intended to guide other deeds. It proposes to have
what the pragmatists call "workings." That is, it
undertakes to guide the life of the one who asserts
the opinion. In that sense, all truth is practical.
If you assert a proposition in mathematics, you
propose to guide the computations, or other synthetic
processes, of whoever is interested in certain mathematical objects. If you say "There is a God,"
and know what you mean by the term "God," you
lay down some sort of rule for such forms of action
as involve a fitting acknowledgment of God's being
and significance. So far, then, I wholly side with the
pragmatists. There is no pure intellect. There is
no genuine insight which does not also exist as a
guide to some sort of action.

Furthermore, the proper "workings" of an assertion, the rational results of the application of this
opinion to life, must, if the assertion is true, agree
with the expectations of the one who defines the
assertion. And these "workings" belong, indeed, to
the realm of actual and concrete experience, be this

experience wholly human, or be it, in some respect,
an experience which is higher and richer than any
merely human experience. Opinions are active appeals to real life—a life to which we are always
seeking to adjust ourselves, and in which we are
always looking to find our place. The quest for
salvation itself is such an effort to adjust our own
life to the world's life. And if the world's life finds
our efforts to define our relation to the world's actual
and perfectly concrete experience inadequate, then
our assertions are in just so far false; they lead in
that case to blundering actions. We fail. And in
such cases our opinions, indeed, "do not work."

All this I myself insist upon. But next I ask you
to note that the very significance of our human life
depends upon the fact that we are always undertaking to adjust ourselves to a life, and to a type of
experience, which, concrete and real though it is,
is never reducible to the terms of any purely human
experience. Were this not the case; were not every
significant assertion concerned with a type and form
of life and of experience which no man ever gets;
were not all our actions guided by ideas and ideals
that can never be adequately expressed in simply human terms; were all this, I say, not the case, then—
neither science nor religion, neither worldly prudence
nor ideal morality, neither natural common-sense
nor the loftiest forms of spirituality would be possible. Here I can only repeat, but now with explicit reference to the active aspect of our opinions

and of our experience, the comments that I made in my former lecture. Man as he is experiences from moment to moment. What is here and now, not future "workings," not past expectations, but the present—this is what he more immediately gets and verifies. These momentary experiences of his, these pains and these data of perception, are what he can personally verify for himself. And to this life in each instant he is confined, so far as his own personal and individual experience is concerned. But man *means*, he *intends*, he *estimates*, he *judges* life, not as it appears to him at any one instant, but as "in the long run," or "for the common-sense of mankind," or as "from a rational point of view" he holds that it ought to be judged. Now I again insist—there is not one of us who ever directly observes in his own person what it is which even the so-called common-sense of mankind is said to verify and find to be true. The experience which "mankind" is said to possess is not merely the mere collection of your momentary feelings or perceptions, or mine. It is a conceived integral experience which no individual man ever gets before him. When we conceive it, we first treat it as something impersonal. If it is personal, the person who gets it before him is greater than any man. Yet unless some such integral experience is as concrete and genuine a fact, as real a life, as any life that you and I from moment to moment lead, then all so-called "common-sense" is meaningless. But if such an integral experience is real, then that by which the pragmatic "workings" of our private and personal opinions are to be tested and are tested is a certain integral whole of life in which we all live and move and have our being, but which is no more the mere heap and collection of our moments of fragmentary experience, and of our vicissitudes of shifting moods, than a symphony is a mere collection of notes on paper, or of scraped strings and quivering tubes, or of air waves, or even of the deeds of separate musicians.

The life, then, the experience, the concrete whole, wherein our assertions have their workings, with which our active ideas are labouring to agree, to which our will endlessly strives to adjust itself, in which we are saved or lost, is a life whose touch with our efforts is as close as its superiority to our merely human narrowness is concretely and actively triumphant whenever our pettiness gets moulded to a higher reasonableness.   And unless such a life above our individual level is real, our human efforts have no sense whatever, and chaos drowns out the meaning of the pragmatists and of the idealists alike. *If one asks, however, by what workings our significant assertions propose to be judged, I answer, by their workings as experienced and estimated from the point of view of such a larger life, as conforming to its will, or falling short thereof, as leading toward or away from our salvation.* For it is just such a larger life by which we all propose and intend to be judged, whenever we make our active appeal to life take the form of any serious assertion whatever. If a man proposes to let his ideas be tested not by his momentary caprice, and not by any momentary datum of experience, but by "what proves to be thèir workings in the long run," then already he is appealing to an essentially superhuman type of empirical test and estimate. For no man taken as this individual ever personally experiences "the long run," that is, the integral course and meaning, the right estimate and working of a long series of experiences and deeds. For a man individually observes now this moment and now that—never their presupposed integration, never their union in a single whole of significant life.

If a man says that the workings of his ideas are to be tested by "scientific experience," then again he appeals not to the verdict of any human observer, but to the integrated and universalised and relatively impersonal and superpersonal synthesis of the results of countless observers.

And so, whatever you regard as a genuine test of the workings of your ideas is some living whole of experience above the level of any one of our individual human lives. To this whole you indeed actively appeal. The appeal is an act of will. And in turn you regard that to which you appeal as an experience which is just as live and concrete as your own, and which carries out its own will in that it snubs or welcomes your efforts with a will as hearty as is your own. For what estimates your deeds,

and gives them their meaning, is a life as genuine as
yours and an activity as real as yours. Pragmatism is perfectly justified in regarding the whole
process as no mere contemplation, no merely restful
or static conformity of passive idea to motionless
insight, but, on the contrary, as a significant inter-
action of life with life and of will with will. But the
more vital the process, the more pragmatic the
test of our active opinions through the conformity
or non-conformity of their purposes to the life
wherein we dwell and have our being, the more
vital becomes the fact that, whether we are saved
or lost, we belong to the world's life, and are part
thereof, while, unless this life is more than merely
human in its rational wealth of concrete meaning,
we mortals have no meaning whatever, and the assertions of common-sense as well as of religion lapse
into absurdity.

VI

In order fairly to estimate aright our relation to
this larger life, we must briefly review the further
thesis upon which recent pragmatism lays so much
stress—the thesis that, since the truth of an opinion
consists in the agreement or disagreement of its empirical workings with their anticipated consequences,
all truth is both temporal and relative and cannot
be either eternal or absolute. Let me then say a
word as to the absoluteness of truth.

The thesis of pragmatism as to the active nature

and the practical meaning of all opinions may be illustrated by a simile that, as I think, well brings out the sense in which, as I hold, pragmatism itself is a true doctrine. Any sincere opinion announces a plan of action whereby we are, in some way, to adjust ourselves for some purpose to a real object. That is, an opinion lays down, in some form, a rule for some sort of conduct. This rule is of course valid only for one who has some specific interest in the object in question. For you can guide action only by appealing to the will of the one whom you guide. This is the pragmatist's view of the nature of all assertions and opinions. And so far, as you already know, I agree with the pragmatist. This account is correct.

This being so, we can, for the sake of a simile, compare any definite opinion to the counsel that a coach may give to a player whom he is directing. The player wants to "play the game." He therefore accepts its rules, and has his interests in what the pragmatists call "the concrete situation." The player, at any point in his training or in his activities as a player, may also accept the coach's guidance, and put himself under the coach's directions. If, hereupon, the player acts in accordance with what the coach ordains, the coach's directions have "workings." Their "workings" are in so far the deeds of the player. These deeds, if the issues of the game are sharply defined, are what we may call hits or misses. That is, each one of them either is what, for the purposes of the game and the player, it ought to be, or else it is not what it ought to be. And each act of the player is a hit or a miss in a perfectly objective sense, as a real deed belonging to a world whose relations are determined by the rules and events of the game and by the purposes of the whole body of players.

Applying the simile to the case of assertions, we may say: An assertion is an act whereby our deeds are provided with a sort of coaching. Life itself is our game. Opinions coach the active will as to how to do its deed. If the opinion is definite enough, and if the active will obeys the coach, the opinion has "workings." These workings are our intelligent deeds, which translate our opinions into new life. If our purposes are definite enough, and if the issues of life are for us sharply defined, these deeds are, with reference to our purposes, either hits or misses, either successful or unsuccessful acts, either steps toward winning or steps toward failure. All this is surely concrete enough. And, in real life, this account applies equally to the practical situations of the workshop or of the market-place, and to the ideas and deeds of a religious man seeking salvation.

But now one of the central facts about life is that every deed once done is *ipso facto* irrevocable. That is, at any moment you perform a given deed or you do not. If you perform it, it is done and cannot be undone. This difference between what is done and what is left undone is, in the real and empirical world, *a perfectly absolute difference.* The opportunity for a given individual deed returns not; for the moment when that individual deed can be done never recurs.   Here is a case where the rational constitution of the whole universe gets into definite relation to our momentary experience.   *And if any one wants to be in touch with the "Absolute"—with that reality which the pragmatists fancy to be peculiarly remote and abstract—let him simply do any individual deed whatever and then try to undo that deed.   Let the experiment teach him what one means by calling reality absolute.   Let the truths which that experience teaches any rational being show him also what is meant by absolute truth.*

For this irrevocable and absolute character of the deed, when once done, rationally determines an equally irrevocable character about the truth or falsity of any act of judgment, of any assertion or opinion, which has actually called in a concrete situation for a given deed, and which therefore has had this individual deed for any part of its intended "workings."   Let us return to the simile of the game.   Suppose the coach to counsel a given deed of the player.   Suppose the player, acting on the coach's advice, to perform that deed, to make that play.   Suppose the play to be a misplay.   The play, once made, cannot be recalled.   It stands, if the rules of the game require it so to stand, on the score. If it stands there, then just *that* item of the score

can never be changed under the rules of the game.
The score is, for the game, absolute and irrevocable.
If the coach counselled that misplay, his counsel
was an error. And just as the player's score cannot
be changed without simply abandoning the rules of
the game, so too the coach's record as a blunderer
is, in respect of this one bit of counsel, unalterable.
Analogous results hold for the player's successful
hits and for the coaching that required them. All
this is no result of abstractions or of bare theory. It
is the result of having the will to play the game. It
is the absolute truth that results from joining definite practical issues.

Returning to life, we must say: If our assertions
have a determinate meaning, they get their concrete
workings through counselling determinate individual
deeds. Each deed, as an individual act, is irrevocable and is absolutely what it is. Our deeds, judged
in the light of a reasonable survey of life—a survey
of life such as that to which, when we form our
opinions, and when we act on our opinions, we intend to appeal—are, for a determinate purpose,
either hits or misses. If the issues of life in question when we act are definite enough, our deeds,
under the rules of the game of life, cannot avoid
this character of being the right deeds or the wrong
deeds for the purpose in question and in view of
their actual place in real life. Whoever so acts that
his deeds are done, as a cant phrase has it, "with a
string attached to them"—that is, whoever regards

his deeds as having only relative reality, as capable
of being recalled if he chooses, is not acting seriously. He is not, as they say, really "playing the
game." And, as a fact, he is trifling with absolute
reality. He is not only not serious; he views real
life as it absolutely is not. For whatever individual
deed he actually does is absolutely irrevocable,
whether he wants to recall it or not. Once done,
it stands eternally on the world's score.

Now I insist, whatever assertion, or opinion, regarded as itself an expression of one's will, has for
its intended working one of these irrevocable deeds,
is in so far forth true, as the individual deed which
it counsels is for the required purpose quite irrevocably a right deed when estimated with reference
to this purpose and to the life into whose score it
enters. That is, the opinion is true in so far as
the working which it counsels is a deed that is
in fact a hit in the chosen game of life under the
rules of that game. And whatever opinion counsels
a deed that, as the working of this opinion, is a miss
in the game of life, is a false opinion. And, so I
insist, *this distinction between the truth and falsity of
an opinion that counsels an individual deed is as
absolute and irrevocable as is the place of the deed when
once done on the score of the game of life.*

Whoever denies this position simply trifles with
the very nature of all individual facts of experience;
trifles also with life and with his own decisive will.
Every serious man does his daily business with an

assurance that, since his deeds are irrevocable, his guiding opinions, that counsel his individual deeds give, in an equally irrevocable way, right or wrong guidance, precisely in so far as they get their workings concretely presented in his deeds. And this view about life is no philosopher's abstraction. It is the only genuinely concrete view. Its contradiction is not merely illogical, but practically inane. I cannot do a deed and then undo it. Therefore I cannot declare it to be for a determinate purpose the right individual deed at this point in life, and then say that I did not really mean that counsel to be taken as simply and therefore absolutely true. Absolute reality (namely, the sort of reality that belongs to irrevocable deeds), absolute truth (namely, the sort of truth that belongs to those opinions which, for a given purpose, counsel individual deeds, when the deeds in fact meet the purpose for which they were intended)—these two are not remote affairs invented by philosophers for the sake of "barren intellectualism." *Such absolute reality and absolute truth are the most concrete and practical and familiar of matters.* The pragmatist who denies that there is any absolute truth accessible has never rightly considered the very most characteristic feature of the reasonable will, namely, that it is always counselling irrevocable deeds, and therefore is always giving counsel that is for its own determinate purpose irrevocably right or wrong precisely in so far as it is definite counsel.

One of the least encouraging features of recent discussion is the prominence and popularity of those philosophical opinions which are always proclaiming their "concrete" and "practical" character, while ignoring the most vital and concrete feature of all voluntary life. For the very essence of the will is that, at every moment of action, it decides absolute issues, because it does irrevocable deeds, and therefore, if intelligent at all, is guided by opinions that are as absolutely true or false as their intended workings are irrevocable. I repeat: If you want to know what an absolute truth is, and what an absolute falsity, do anything whatever, and then try to undo your deed. You will find that the opinion which should counsel you to regard it as capable of being undone gives you simply and absolutely false coaching as to any game of life whatever. Every effort to undo your deed is a blunder. Every opinion that you can undo is a trivial and absolutely false absurdity. Just such triviality and absurdity belong to the thesis that absolute truth is an unpractical and inaccessible abstraction.

VII

If, with such a view of the nature of absolute truth, we turn back to estimate the sense in which our opinions about the world as a whole can be true or false, we now see that our account both of the insight of the reason, and of the nature of the world, has become enriched by this whole analysis of the nature of opinion. *Opinions about the universe are counsels as to how to adjust your deeds to the purposes and requirements which a survey of the whole of the life whereto your life belongs shows to be the genuinely rational purposes and requirements.* Every such opinion then, whether true or false, is an effort to adjust your will and your conduct to the intents of a supreme will which decides values, establishes the rule of life, estimates purposes in the light of complete insight. That is, the insight to which your opinions appeal is indeed the insight of a real being who values, estimates, establishes, decides, as concretely as you do, and who is therefore not only all-wise, but possessed of a will. Your search for salvation is a seeking to adjust yourself to this supreme will. That such a will is real is as true as it is true that any opinion whatever which you can form with regard to the real world is either true or false. However ignorant you are, you are, then, in constant touch with the master of life; for you are constantly doing irrevocable deeds whose final value, whose actual and total success or failure, can only be real, or be known, from the point of view of the insight that faces the whole of real life, and with reference to the purposes of the will whose expression is the entire universe.

If, however, you say, with the pragmatists: "There is no whole world, there is no complete view, there is no will that wills the world; for all is temporal, and time flows, and novelties constantly appear, and the world is just now incomplete, and therefore there is nothing eternal," then my answer is perfectly definite. Of course there is, *just at this point of time,* no complete world. Of course, every new deed introduces novelties into the temporal world. But, on the other hand, even to assert this is to assert *that the future, and in fact all the future, in all its individual detail, belongs to reality, and forms part of its wholeness.* To admit this is to admit that the true insight, and the divine will, require, and get, *the endless whole of future time, as well as of past time, before them in one, not timeless, but time-inclusive survey, which embraces the whole of real life.* And just such a survey, and just such a life, not timeless, but time-inclusive, constitute the eternal, which is real, not apart from time, and from our lives, but in, and through and above all our individual lives. The divine will wills in us and in all this world, with its endless past and its endless future, at once. The divine insight is not lifeless. It includes and surveys all life. All is temporal in its ceaseless flow and in its sequence of individual deeds. All is eternal in the unity of its meaning.

To assert this, I insist, is not to deny our freedom and our initiative. The divine will wills me, precisely in so far as it wills that, in each of my individual deeds, I should then and there express my own unique, and in so far free, choice. And to assert, as I do, that the divine will wills all "at once" is not to assert that it wills all *at any one moment of time*, but only that the divine will is expressed in the totality of its deeds that are done in all moments of time.

But this, you will say, is still philosophy, not what the plain man needs for his religion. The question remains: Through what source of insight are we able to adjust our daily lives to this divine wisdom and to this divine will? I answer: Through a source of insight which is accessible to the plainest and simplest reasonable and sincere human being. Yet this source of insight, not yet expressly named in our study, includes in a beautiful and spiritual unity the true sense of our individual experience, of our social experience, of our reason, and of our will, and gives us at length a genuine religion. This new source we are to study in our next lecture.

V

THE RELIGION OF LOYALTY

V

THE RELIGION OF LOYALTY

Our first two lectures dealt with sources of religious insight well known to all of you, however unsatisfactory you may have found them. Our third and fourth lectures have led us into philosophical discussions which many of you will have found neither satisfactory nor familiar. And so, in imagination, I can hear you declaring that, if the foregoing sources of insight are indeed all that we have, religious truth seems still very far away. "The saints," I hear you saying, "may comfort us when they tell us of their personal and private intuitions; but they perplex us with the conflicting variety of their experiences. The social enthusiasts undertake to show us the way to salvation through love; but the world of men in which they bid us seek the divine is a world that is by nature as much in need of salvation as we ourselves are. The sages point to the starry heaven of reason which, as they insist, overarches us; but this heaven seems cold; and its stars appear far away from our needy life. And if, replying to this very objection, and, incidentally, replying also to the doctrine of the pragmatists,

somebody insists that this heavenly world of the
reason is also an expression of the living divine will,
we still remember that our deepest need is to see
how the divine will may be done on earth as it is in
heaven.   And this is what we have not yet learned
to see.   The foregoing sources then appear to leave
us, after all, with no vital and positive religion."

I

Thus some of you may at this point express your
discontent. If you do, I find this discontent justified.   If the foregoing lectures had indeed exhausted
the account of the accessible sources of religious insight, we should be hopeless of finding any religion
that could satisfy at once the individual need for
salvation, the social requirement that we should seek
for salvation through union with our brethren, the
rational demand for a coherent view of truth, and
the aim of the will to conform itself to the laws of
the master of life with whom we need to be united.
In other words, all of the foregoing sources of insight, considered as separate sources, present to us
problems which they do not solve, and leave the
real nature of the saving process clouded by mists
of ignorance.   What we most need at this point is
some source of insight which shall show how to
unite the lessons that the preceding sources have
furnished.   The present lecture must be devoted to
an account of such a source.   I should be quite

helpless to engage in this new undertaking were it not for the fact that the spiritual life of humanity's best servants and friends has long since shown us how to overcome the difficulties by which our present inquiry is, at this point, beset. These friends and servants of mankind have used, in fact, that source of insight which I mentioned in the closing words of the last lecture, a source by means of which the results and the moving principles of individual experience, of social experience, of reason, and of will are brought into a certain creative unity to which the noblest spiritual attainments of our world are due. We shall return, therefore, in this lecture, from speculation to life; and our guides will be, not the philosophers, nor yet the geniuses of the inarticulate religious intuitions, but those who, while they indeed possess intuitions and thoughts, also actually live in the spirit.

Nevertheless, for our purpose, the foregoing method of approaching our topic has been, I hope, justified. We wish to know the sources and to see what each is worth. We must therefore consider each source in its distinction from the others. Then only can we see what brings them together in the higher religious life. We must reflect where religion itself wins its way without reflection. Had we begun our study where this lecture begins, with the effort to understand at once this new source of insight, we should have been less able than we now are to discern the motives that enter into its con-

stitution and to appreciate its accomplishments.
We have had to emphasise difficulties in order to
prepare the way for our study of that source of insight which, in the history of humanity's struggles
toward the light, has best enabled men to triumph
over these difficulties.

This new source has come into the lives of men in
intimate connection with their efforts to solve the
problem not merely of religion, in our present sense
of the word, but also of duty.   I shall therefore first
have to tell you how the problem of duty is distinguished from the problem of religion.   Then I
shall show you how the effort to solve each of these
problems has thrown light upon the other.

Duty and religion have, in the minds of all of
you, close relations.   Both have to do with our
ideals, with our needs, with the conforming of our
lives to our ideals, and with the attainment of some
sort of good.   Yet you also well know that these
relations of duty and of morality on the one hand,
of religion and of salvation on the other, are not
relations easy to define with entire clearness.   Some
men in our age, as you know, tell you that they are
unable, in their present state of mind, to get much
help from religion.   And some men who insist that
the religious problems have for them no solution
whatever, are ardently and sincerely dutiful in
spirit.   On the other hand, there are those who, in
their own minds, are so sure of salvation that they
actually make light of the call of duty, or at least

see little that is saving in the thought of duty. In the opinion of very many, no effort to lead a dutiful life can lead to salvation unless some sort of divine grace, which is a free gift from above, intervenes to accomplish the saving process. Meanwhile, there are those who declare not only that the dutiful life tends of itself to lead to salvation, but that the persistent doing of our duty is precisely the whole of what constitutes salvation.

You will readily see that the plan of these lectures forbids any direct study of the Pauline doctrine regarding the relation of faith to works, of divine grace to human dutifulness. The mere mention of St. Paul, however, side by side with the reminder that, at many times in history, and especially to-day, there are those for whom, despite Paul's teaching as to the vanity of mere works, there is no religion but the religion of duty, will serve to show that serious questions are here involved, and that the true relations between religion and morality are by no means self-evident.

Let me briefly distinguish between the religious interest and the moral interest. Then we may be able to recognise how closely they are related, and yet how far, under certain conditions, they may drift apart, and how sharply they may sometimes come to be opposed.

II

There is an obvious contrast between the points of view from which morality and religion consider the problem of life. Whatever may be your views as to what your duty is, it is plain that the moral interest centres about this idea of duty. That is, the moral interest seeks to define right deeds and to insist that they shall be done. It estimates the rightness of deeds with reference to some ideal of life. But however it conceives this ideal, it makes its main appeal to the active individual. It says: "Do this." The religious interest, on the other hand, centres about the sense of need, or, if it is successful in finding this need satisfied, it centres about the knowledge of that which has delivered the needy from their danger. It appeals for help, or waits patiently for the Lord, or rejoices in the presence of salvation. It therefore may assume any one of many different attitudes toward the problem of duty. It may seek salvation through deeds, or again it may not, in the minds of some men, appeal to the active nature in any vigorous way whatever. Some religious moods are passive, contemplative, receptive, adoring rather than strenuous. It is therefore quite consistent with the existence of a religious interest to feel suspicious of the dutiful restlessness of many ardent souls.

"They also serve who only stand and wait."

Such is sometimes the comforting, sometimes the warning word that seems to many to express the religious interest.

This general contrast between the two interests assumes many special forms when we consider how moralists—that is, teachers who especially emphasise the call of duty—may stand related to the two postulates upon which, as we have seen, the higher religions base their appeal. Religion, in our sense of the word, depends upon asserting: (1) That there is some one highest end of existence, some goal of life, some chief good; and (2) That, by nature, man is in great danger of completely failing to attain this good, so that he needs to be saved from this danger.

Now the first of these two postulates religion has frequently, although not always, shared with the moralists, that is, with those who devote themselves to teaching us how to act rightly. Aristotle, for instance, based his ethical doctrine (one of the most influential books in the history of morals) upon the postulate that there is a highest good. Many others who have discussed or have preached morality, have asserted that all obligations are subject to one ultimate obligation, which is the requirement to act with reference to the highest good. Yet this agreement as to the highest good turns out to be not quite universal when one compares the opinions of the teachers of religion, on the one hand, and of the moralists on the other. Popular and traditional morality often takes the form of a little hoard of

maxims about right acts—maxims whose relations
to one another, and to any one highest goal of life,
remain obscure. Each maxim is supposed to define
a duty. Of course it also tells us how to win some
special good or how to avoid some particular evil.
But what this special duty has to do with winning
any one highest good is not thus made explicit.
And since many who make traditional morality
prominent in their minds and lives are unaware of
the deeper spirit that indeed, as I hold, underlies
every serious endeavour, these persons simply remain unconscious that their morality has any religious motive or that they are dealing with the problem of salvation. Even some professional teachers
of duty are mere legalists who do not succeed in
reducing the law which they teach to any rational
unity. And for such people the postulate which
religion makes the head of the corner is rather a
stumbling-stone. They doubt or question whether
there is any highest good whatever or any pearl of
great price. Yet they illustrate the essential feature of morality by insisting that certain deeds must
be done.

But, however it may be with the first of the religious postulates, it is the second (the postulate that
we are naturally in very great danger of missing the
true goal of life) which leaves open the greater room
for differences of interest as between the religious
teachers and the teachers of duty. Suppose that
we are in agreement in holding that there is a highest

good. Nevertheless, the question: How far is man naturally in danger of missing this supreme goal? is a question which, since we are all fallible mortals, leaves room for many varieties of opinion. How I myself view the matter, I told you in our first lecture. And to me the religious need seems an insistent and clear need. But many moralists are partisans of duty as a substitute for religion. And they are often much more optimistic regarding human nature than I am. In their opinion the goal can be reached, or at least steadily approached, by simple dutifulness in conduct, without any aid from other motives that should tend to our salvation.

There is, then, a pearl of great price. But—so such teachers hold—why sell all that you have to buy that pearl, when by nature you are able to win it through a reasonable effort? Dutifulness is the name for the spirit that leads to such an effort. And dutifulness, say these teachers, is as natural as any other normal function. "No general catastrophe threatens our destiny," they insist. "Why not do right? That is in your own personal power and is sufficient for your deepest need. You need cry out for no aid from above. You can be saved if you choose. There is no dark problem of salvation."

To such optimists the intensely religious often respond with that strange horror and repugnance which only very close agreement can make possible. Near spiritual kin can war together with a bitterness that mutual strangers cannot share. In this case,

as you see, the goal is the same for both parties to
the controversy. Both want to reach some highest
good. The cheerful optimists simply feel sure of
being able to reach, through action, what the ear-
nestly devout are passionately seeking by the aid of
faith. Yet each side may regard the other with a
deep sense of sacred aversion. "Fanatic!" cries the
partisan of duty to his religious brother. "Mere
moralist," retorts the other, and feels that no ill
name could carry more well-founded opprobrium.
The issue involved is indeed both delicate and
momentous.

The same issue may become only graver in its
intensity when, in a given case, a religious man and
a moralist agree as to *both* of the main postulates of
religion, so that for both there is a highest good to
seek and a great peril to avoid. For now the question arises: What way leads to salvation?

Suppose that the answer to this question seems,
at any point in the development of human insight,
simply doubtful. Suppose mystery overhangs the
further path that lies before both the religious inquirer and the moralist. In such a case the religious interest meets at least a temporary defeat.
The religious inquirer must acknowledge that he
is baffled. But just this defeat of the religious interest often seems to be the moralist's opportunity.
"You cannot discover your needed superhuman
truths," he then says. "You cannot touch heaven.
You remain but a man. But at all events you can

do a man's work, however hard that work is, however opposed it is to your natural sloth and degradation, however great the danger of perdition. Perhaps nobody knows the way of salvation. But a man can know and can daily do each day's duty. He does not know how to attain the goal. But he knows what the goal is, and it is better to die striving for the goal than to live idly gazing up into heaven." In such a case, even if the moralist fully recognises the depth of our need of salvation, and the greatness of the danger, still the strenuous pursuit of duty often seems to him to be a necessary substitute for religion. And then the moralist may regard his own position as the only one that befits a truth-loving man; and the religious interests, which appear to fix the attention upon remote and hopeless mysteries, may seem to him hindrances to the devoted moral life. Against all dangers and doubts he hurls his "everlasting No." His only solution lies in strenuousness. He is far from the Father's house. He knows not even whether there is any father or any home of the spirit. But he proposes to face the truth as it is, and to die as a warrior dies, fighting for duty.

But of course quite a different outcome is, for many minds, the true lesson of life. The religious man may come to feel sure that the way of salvation is indeed known to him; but it may seem to him a way that is opened not through the efforts of moral individuals, but only through the workings

of some divine power that, of its own moving, elects
to save mankind.   In this case the classic doctrine
that grace alone saves, and that, without such grace,
works are but ˌvanity, is, in one form or another,
emphasised by religious teachers in their controversies with the moralists.   The history of Christianity illustrates several types of doctrine according to which divine grace is necessary to salvation,
so that mere morality not only cannot save, but of
itself even tends to insure perdition.   And in the
history of Northern Buddhism there appear teachings closely analogous to these evangelical forms
of Christianity.   So the religious interests here in
question are very human and wide-spread.   Whoever thus views the way of salvation can in fact
appeal to vast bodies of religious experience, both
individual and social, to support his opposition
against those who see in the strenuous life the only
honest mode of dealing with our problem.   Whoever
has once felt, under any circumstances, his helpless-
ness to do right knows what such religious experience of the need of grace means.   Hence it is easy
to see how the earnest followers of a religion may
condemn those moralists who agree with them both
as to the need and as to the dangers of the natural
man.   In fact the two parties may condemn each
other all the more because both accept the two postulates upon which the quest for salvation is based.

Yet even these are not the only forms in which
this tragic conflict amongst brethren often appears.

I must mention still another form. Suppose that, in the opinion of the followers of some religion, not only the knowledge of the way of salvation is open, but also the attainment of the goal, the entering into rest, the fruition, is, for the saints or for the enlightened, an actual experience. There is, then, such a thing as a complete winning of the highest good. So the faithful may teach. Hereupon the moralists may adopt the phrase which James frequently used in opposing those who seemed to themselves to be in actual touch with some absolute Being. The only use of the opinion of such people, James in substance said, is that it gives them a sort of "moral holiday." For James, quite erroneously, as I think, supposed that whoever believed the highest good to be in any way realised in the actual world, was thereby consciously released from the call of duty, and need only say:

> "God's in his heaven,
> All's right with the world."

In such a world, namely, there would be, as James supposed, nothing for a righteous man to do. The alternative that perhaps the only way whereby God can be in his heaven, or all right with the world, is the way that essentially includes the doing of strenuous deeds by righteous men, James persistently ignored, near as such an alternative was to the spirit of his own pragmatism.

Nevertheless, it is true that there have indeed

been, amongst the religiously minded, many who
have conceived the highest good merely in the form
of some restful communion with the master of life,
merely as tranquillity in the presence of God, or
merely as a contemplative delight in some sort of
beauty. And it is true that some of these have
said: "The saints, or at all events the enlightened,
even in the present life, do enter into this rest.
And for them there is indeed nothing left to do."
To such, of course, the moralists may reply: "You
enlightened ones seem to think yourselves entitled
to a 'moral holiday.' We strenuous souls reject
your idleness as unworthy of a man. Your religion
is a barren æstheticism, and is so whether it takes
the outward form of an ascetic and unworldly contemplation or assumes the behaviour of a company
of highly cultivated pleasure-seekers who delight
in art merely for art's sake and know nothing of
duty." To such believers in salvation through mere
attainment of peace, James's criticism rightly applies. In these lectures, as I ask you to note, I
have never defined salvation in such terms. Salvation includes triumph and peace, but peace only
in and through the power of the spirit and the life
of strenuous activity.

But such partisans of the religion of spiritual idleness as I have mentioned may nevertheless return
the moralist's scorn with scorn. If they are advo-
cates of art for art's sake, of mere beauty as the
highest good, they find the restlessness of the moral-

ists hectic or barbarous. If they are mystical quiet-
ists, they regard mere moralism as the struggling of
a soul that is not saved. If moral endeavour were
the last word, they insist, we should all of us be in
the Hades of Sisyphus. And no doubt their scorn,
even if ill-founded, deserves consideration. For
even the most one-sided emphasis upon any aspect
of spiritual truth is instructive, if only your eyes
are open.

Such are some of the ways in which, in the course
of human history, the religiously minded and the
moralists have been divided. To sum up: Certain
of the lovers of religion have, upon occasion, condemned moralists, sometimes as legalists who do not
know that there is any highest good, sometimes as
vain optimists who ignore the danger of perdition,
sometimes as despisers of divine grace, sometimes
as the barbarous troublers of spiritual peace. Certain moralists, in their turn, and according as they
ignore or accept the postulates upon which the
religious interest is based, have condemned the devout, sometimes as the slanderers of our healthy
human nature, sometimes as seekers in the void for
a light that does not shine, sometimes as slavish
souls who hope to get from grace gifts that they
have not the courage to earn for themselves, sometimes as idlers too fond of "moral holidays." And,
as moralists, their common cry has been, ever since
the times of Amos: "Woe unto those who are at
ease in Zion."

We have reviewed, then, some of these conflicts. I hope that you see upon what general issue they all alike turn. The moralists are essentially the partisans of action. They seek a good. But their great postulate is that there is something right for us to do. Therefore the issue is that between our need of something not ourselves to save us and our power to win a greater or lesser good through our own moral activity. Whoever so exclusively emphasises the fact that the divine is not of our making, and that its ways are not our ways, and that its good is something beyond our power to create or attain of ourselves—whoever, I say, so exclusively emphasises these things that he makes light of our efforts to attain the good somewhere comes into conflict with moralists. Whoever, as moralist, so exclusively appeals to our own energies that he seems to hold that our duty would be just as much our duty, "If we were alone upon the earth and the gods blind," somewhere meets the religious opponent who mocks his pride, or despises his restlessness, or laments his contempt for the divine grace.

Now these conflicts are, I insist, no merely speculative controversies. They play a great part in history. They have darkened countless lives. And they grow out of motives deep in human nature. What is here most important for us is that they point us toward our new source of insight. What a narrower way of living can divide, a deeper and truer mode of living can unite. Our problem assumes a new form. Is there any mode of living that is just *both* to the moral and to the religious motives? Is there any way of reconciling our need of a grace that shall save with the call of the moral life that we shall be strenuous in the pursuit of our duty?

Let us here approach this problem from the side of our moral consciousness. For at this point we are already familiar with the religious need. Does there exist amongst men a type of morality that, in and for itself, is already essentially religious, so that it knows nothing of this conflict between duty and religion? I reply, there is such a type of morality. There is a sort of consciousness which equally demands of those whom it inspires, spiritual attainment and strenuousness, serenity and activity, resignation and vigour, life in the spirit and ceaseless enterprise in service. Is this form of consciousness something belonging only to highly and intellectually cultivated souls? Is it the fruit of abstract thinking alone? Is it the peculiar possession of the philosophers? Or, on the other hand, does it arise solely through dumb and inarticulate intuitions? Is it consistent only with a highly sensitive and mystical temperament? Does it belong only to the childhood of the spirit? Is it exclusively connected with the belief in some one creed? To all these questions I reply: No.

This sort of consciousness is possessed in a very

high degree by some of the humblest and least
erudite of mankind. Those in whose lives it is a
notable feature may be personally known only to
a few near friends. But the spirit in which they
live is the most precious of humanity's possessions.
And such people may be found belonging to all the
ages in which we can discover any genuinely humane
activities, and to all those peoples that have been
able to do great work, and to all the faiths that contain any recognisable element of higher religious
significance.

III

I can best show you what I mean by next very
briefly reviewing the motives upon which the idea
of duty itself rests, and by then showing to what,
upon the noblest level of human effort, these motives lead.

Our moral interests have a development which,
in all its higher phases, runs at least parallel to the
development of our religious interests, even in cases
where the two sorts of interests seem to clash. The
moral problems arise through certain interactions
that take place between our individual and our
social experience. The reason reviews these interactions and takes interest in unifying our plan of
life. The will is always, from the very nature of
the case, concerned in the questions that here arise.
For whatever else morality is, it is certain that your
morality has to do with your conduct, and that

moral goodness cannot be yours unless your will itself is good. Wealth might come to you as a mere gift of fortune. Pleasure might be brought to you from without, so far as you have the mere capacity for pleasure. The same might appear to be true even in case of salvation, if, indeed, salvation is wholly due to saving grace. But moral goodness, if you can get it at all, requires your active cooperation. You can earn it only in case you do something to possess it. Its motto reads: "*Erwirb es um es zu besitzen.*"

Therefore the moral question always takes the form of asking: What am I to do? The first contribution to the answer is furnished, upon all levels of our self-consciousness, by our individual experience. And one apparently simple teaching that we get from this source may be stated in a maxim which wayward people often insist upon, but which only the very highest type of morality can rationally interpret: "I am to do what I choose, in case only I know what I choose and am able to do it." From this point of view, my only limitations, at first sight, seem to be those set for me by my physical weakness. There are many things that, if I had the power, I should or might choose to do. But since I frequently cannot accomplish my will, I must learn to limit myself to what I can carry out. So far, I say, our individual experience, if taken as our sole moral guide, seems at first to point out the way.

But this first teaching of our individual experience is by no means so simple as it seems. For the question arises: What is it, on the whole, that I choose to do? And, as we saw very early in these discussions, each of us is by nature so full of caprices and of various aims, that, left to ourselves, we live not only narrowly but inconsistently. Hence we spend much of our lives in finding out, after the fact, that what we chose to do at one moment of our lives has hopelessly thwarted what we intended to do at some other moment. Self-will then, left to itself, means self-defeat. That is the lesson of life. And the question: What is it that, on the whole, I would choose to do if I had the power? is a question that individual experience, taken by itself, never answers in any steadily consistent way. Therefore, as we all sooner or later come to see, one of our most persistent limitations is *not* our physical weakness to accomplish what we choose, but our incapacity, when left to ourselves, to find out what it is that we propose and really choose to do. Therefore, just because individual experience, taken by itself, never gives steady guidance, we have to look elsewhere for a rule.

The question: What am I to do? is never in practice answered without consulting, more or less persistently, our social experience. Being what we are, naturally gregarious, imitative, and, when trained, conventional creatures, who, indeed, often fight with our kind, but who also love our kind, who not only cannot bear to be too much alone, but are simply helpless when wholly isolated from our fellows (unless we have already learned in their company the very arts that we may be able to use while we are alone), we can give no answer to the question: What is to be my choice? without pretty constantly consulting our social interests. And these interests are indeed plentiful and absorbing. But they too are naturally conflicting. And so, taken as they come, they give us no rule of life.

To be sure, the social will in general says to us: "Live with your fellows, for you cannot do without them. Learn from them how to live; for you have to live more or less in their way. Imitate them, co-operate with them, at least enough to win such ideas as will help you to know what you want and such skill as will make you best able to accomplish whatever, in view of your social training, you are led to choose. Do not oppose them too much, for they are many, and, if stirred up against you, can easily destroy you. Conform, then, to their will enough to get power to have your own way." And so far our ordinary social will gives us more or less consistent counsel. But beyond such really rather barren advice (the counsel of an inane worldly prudence), our social experience, as it daily comes to us, has no single ideal to furnish, no actually universal rules to lay down. For, as I go about in social relations, sometimes I love my fellows and sometimes I feel antipathy for them. Sometimes

I am full of pity for their woes and long to help them. Sometimes they are my rivals; and I then naturally try to crush them. There is thus no one social tendency that, as it comes to us in the course of our ordinary social experience, gives us sufficient guidance to tell us how to escape self-defeat. For my love and pity war with my social greed and with my rivalries. I am so far left to my chaos.

Thus, then, if I sum up my position, I indeed propose to do what I choose, in so far as I am able, and in so far as I can find out what it is that I choose and can avoid thwarting myself by my own choices. And the art of learning how to choose, and what to choose, and how to carry out my will, is for me, since I am gregarious, imitative, and conventionalised, a social art. But, on the other hand, no social art that I ordinarily learn is sufficient either to teach me my whole purpose in life, or to make a consistent self of me, or to lead me out of that chaos of self-thwarting efforts wherein so many men pass their lives.

IV

You already know, from our former discussion, how our reason views the situation thus created by this chaos of social and of individual interests. How real and how confused this chaos is, the daily record of certain aspects of the ordinary social life of men which you see in each morning's newspaper may serve to illustrate. These princes and peoples, these rebels and executioners, these strikers and employers, these lovers and murderers, these traders and bankrupts, these who seem for the moment to triumph and these who just now appear to be ground under the opponent's or the oppressor's heel, what arts of living were they and are they all following? Well, each in his way appears to have been choosing to have his own will; yet each, being a social creature, had learned from his fellows all his vain little arts of life. Each loved some of his fellows and was the rival of others. Each had his standards of living, standards due to some more or less accidental and unstable union of all the motives thus barely suggested. The news of the day tells you how some of these won their aims, for the moment, while others were thwarted. What I ask you to note, and what the reason of every man in his more enlightened moments shows him, is that each of these who at any moment was thwarted, precisely in so far as he had any will of his own at all, was defeated not only by his fellows, but by himself. For this special will of his was some caprice not large enough to meet his own ends. The career, for instance, of that man who failed in love or in business or in politics is wrecked. His reputation is lost. Well, it was his will, as a social being, to aim at just such a career and to value just that sort of reputation. Had he chosen to be a hermit, or a saint, or a Stoic, what would just such

a career and such a reputation have been to him?
How could he have lost unless he had sought?
And his failure, to what was it due? No doubt to
some choice of his own quite as much as to his
rival's skill. He wanted freedom to carry on his
own speculations. He got that freedom and lost
his fortune. He wanted to be free to choose whom
and how to love. He had his way and defeated
his own aim. He chose to follow his ambitions.
They have led him where he is.

Such are perfectly reasonable reflections upon the
course of ordinary social conflicts. They suggest
to our more considerate moments the very sort of
reflection which, at the outset of the present discussion, led us to define the religious ideal of salvation. Only now this type of reflection appears as
aiming to lead us to some practical rule for guiding
our active life. For our attention is now fixed, not
on a condition to be called salvation, but on a rule
for doing something in accordance with our own
true will. This rule is, negatively stated, the following: Do *not* seek, either in your individual self
as you are or in your social experience as it comes,
for the whole truth either about what your own
will is or about how you can get your aims. For
if you confine yourself to such sources of moral insight, you will go on thwarting yourself quite as
genuinely, even if by good luck, not quite as scan-
dalously, as the bankrupt speculators and the strikers and the outcast oppressors, and the politicians

and the murderers, and the deposed monarchs and the defeated revolutionists, of whom you read in the newspapers, have thwarted both their individual and their social will. In brief: Put not your trust in caprices, either individual or social. On the positive side, the rule here in question is: In order to find out what is your true choice, and how you can live without thwarting yourself, make your *principle* of life such that whatever fortune besets you, you can inwardly say: "I have not really failed, for I have acted as I intended, and also as I still intend to act, and have had my will whatever the consequences that fortune has brought to me, or however my momentary mood happens to change, or however this or that social caprice leads men to love or to despise me." Such is the moral insight that the first use of your reason, in thus reviewing life, suggests. Or, as the moral common-sense of the wise has often stated the rule here in question: So act that, upon any calm review of the sense of your individual and of your social life, you shall never have ground to regret the principle of your action, never have ground to say: "By choosing thus I thwarted my own will."

As you hear these statements, I hope that, reduced to their very lowest terms: "*So act as never to have reason to regret the principle of your action,*" they express a sort of counsel for life which is not strange to common-sense, even if it has received an abstract expression in the famous ethical philosophy of Kant.

Only, as you will rightly insist, this counsel is indeed
a seemingly hopeless counsel of perfection when it
is addressed to the natural man, who merely has
taken his instincts as he found them developing,
and his social world as he has felt it fascinating or
disturbing him, and who has then stumbled on,
more or less prudently and obstinately trying to
find out what it really is that he wants to do in life.
Such a man will cry out: "But how shall I discover
a principle of life such that, if I hold thereto, I
shall never, upon any reasonable survey of life,
regret following that principle?"

V

Here at length let life itself answer the question.
As I was preparing these very words, and thinking
what new instance to choose, in order to illustrate
afresh the very principle that I have in mind, the
newspaper of the day, side by side with its usual
chronicle of unreason and of disaster, reported the
approaching end of a public servant. This public
servant was Ida Lewis, who for fifty years was the
official keeper of the Lime Rock lighthouse in Narra-
gansett Bay. She had been known for more than
fifty years for her early and later often-repeated
heroism as a life-saver. And now she was at last
on her death-bed. She has since died. I know
nothing of her career but what public reports have
told. So far as her duty required her at her post,

she kept her light burning through all the nights and the storms of those many years. She saved, in all, upon various occasions, eighteen lives of those who were in danger from wreck. Her occupation thus had its perils. It had, what must have been much harder to endure, its steady call upon daily fidelity. It was, on the whole, an obscure and humble occupation; although by chance, as well as by reason of her skill and devotion, this particular lighthouse keeper was privileged to become in a sense famous. But certainly it could have been no part of her original plan to pursue a famous career. When we seek public prominence we do not select the calling of the lighthouse keeper. I do not know how she came to find this calling. She may not even have chosen it. But she certainly chose how to live her life when she had found it. What it means for the world to have such lives lived, a very little thought will show us. What spirit is needed to live such lives as they should be lived, we seldom consider, until such a public servant, dying with the fruits of her years to some extent known to the public, reminds us of our debt and of her devotion.

The newspaper in which I read of this case, in commenting upon its significance, also reported (I do not know how accurately), this incident, of which some of you may know more than I do. I quote the words:[1]

"Forty-one years ago, Daniel Williams, keeper of

[1] *Boston Evening Transcript*, October 23, 1911.

the light at Little Traverse Bay, in Lake Michigan,
went out in a boat for the rescue of a ship's crew in
distress, and did not come back alive. For three
days the storm continued. But his sorrowing
widow did not forget other lives, and each night
climbed the winding stairs and trimmed the lamp.
This duty she discharged until the government
learned the situation, when it authorised her to
continue. And she is still at her post."

Lighthouse keepers are not the only people who
live thus. There are countless lights kept alive in
homes where want or weariness or stormy sorrow
have long since and often entered, and have again
and again seemed about to overwhelm, but where,
after many years, faithful souls, well known to many
of you, are, despite fortune, still at their post, with
the light burning.

And now, I ask you, What is the spirit which
rules such lives? It is a spirit which is familiar in
song and story; for men always love to tell about
it when they meet with impressive examples of its
workings. What I regret is that, when men repeat
such songs and stories, familiarity breeds, not indeed
contempt (for our whole nature rejoices to think
of such deeds), but a certain tendency to false emphasis. We notice the dramatic and heroic incidents of such lives, and are charmed with the pic-
turesque or with the thrilling features of the tale.
And so we seem to ourselves to be dealing mainly
with anecdotes and with accidents. We fail suffi-

ciently to consider that back of the exceptional show
of heroism there has to be the personal character,
itself the result of years of devotion and of training—
the character that has made itself ready for these
dramatic but, after all, not supremely significant
opportunities. Only when we in mind run over
series of such cases do we see that we are dealing
with a spirit suited not only to great occasions, but
to every moment of reasonable life, and not only to
any one or two callings, but to all sorts and conditions of men.

The spirit in question is the one which is often
well illustrated in the lives of warriors who willingly
face death for their flag—if only they face death
not merely as brutes may also face it (because their
fighting blood is aroused), but as reasonable men
face death who clearly see what conditions make it
"man's perdition to be safe." There are two tests
by which we may know whether the warriors really
have the spirit of which I am speaking, namely, the
spirit that was also, and quite equally, present in
the widow who, in all the agony of a new grief, and
through the storm that had taken away her husband, still climbed the lonely stairway and trimmed
the lamp which he could never again tend. The
first test that the warrior and the lighthouse tender
are moved by the same spirit is furnished by the fact
that those warriors who are rightly filled with this
spirit are as well able to live by it in peace as in
war; are, for instance, able even to surrender to

the foe, when fortune and duty require them to do
so—to surrender, I say, with the same calm dignity
and unbroken courage that Lee showed in his interview with Grant at Appomattox, and that inspired him in the years of defeat and of new toils
through which he had still to live after the war.
That is, the warrior, if rightly inspired, is as ready
for life as for death, is as ready for peace as for war;
and despises defeat as much as danger—fearing only
sloth and dishonour and abandonment of the service.   The other test is whether the warrior is ready
to recognise and to honour, with clear cordiality, this
same spirit when it is manifested in another calling,
or in another service, and, in particular, is manifested by his enemy.   For then the warrior knows
that warfare itself is only the accident of fortune,
and that the true spirit of his own act is one which
could be manifested without regard to the special occasion that has required him to face death just here
or to fight on this side.   If the spirit of the warrior
bears these tests, his faithfulness is of the type that
could be shown as well by the lonely light-tender
in her grief as by the hero for whom glory waits.

And again, this spirit is the very one that martyrs
have shown when they died for their faith; that
patient mothers and fathers, however obscure and
humble, show when they toil, in true devotion, for
their homes; that lovers mean to express when
they utter such words as the ones which we earlier
quoted from Mrs. Browning.   And lest all these

instances should impress you with the idea that the spirit in question has to do only with brilliant emotional colourings, such as those which fill our imaginations when we think of war, and of brave deaths, and of heroic triumph over grief, and of lovers' vows, let me turn at once to what some of you may think to be the other extreme of life. Let me say that, to my mind, the calm and laborious devotion to a science which has made possible the life-work of a Newton, or of a Maxwell, or of a Darwin is still another example, and a very great example, of this same spirit—an example full of the same strenuousness, the same fascinated love of an idealised object, and, best of all, full of the willingness to face unknown fortunes, however hard, and to abandon, when that is necessary, momentary joys, however dear, in a pursuit of one of the principal goods which humanity needs—namely, an understanding of the wonderful world in which we mortals are required to work out our destiny. It is not a superficial resemblance that the lighthouse tender and the scientific man both seek to keep and to spread light for the guidance of men.

The lighthouse tender, the mother, the warrior, the patriot, the martyr, the true lover, the scientific investigator—they all may show, I insist, this same essential spirit.

> "Patient through the watches long,
> Serving most with none to see;"

superior to fortune because something that is worthier than any fortune seems to call them to their task. Such are undismayed in defeat. So Newton was undismayed when he looked for the needed confirmation of his theory in the motion of the moon and for the time failed. He worked on steadily, without any effort to win renown by hasty publication of possible explanations, until new advances of science showed why confirmation had so far been lacking and brought him what he needed. So Lee turned to the new life after the war. So the widow climbed the lonely stairway, despite her lost one, and because of her lost one. So the martyrs faced the lions. These all were sustained through long toil, or bewildering grief, by a spirit that tended to make them masters of their own lives and to bring them into unity with the master of all life.

We have illustrated the spirit. We now ask: What is the principle which dominates such lives? Is it or is it not a principle such, that one at any time wholly devoted to it could thereafter, upon a reasonable review of life, wisely regret having chosen to live thus? If it is not such a principle, if on the contrary it is a principle such that any reasonable view of life approves it, let us know what it is, let us detach it from the accidental conditions which at once adorn and disguise it for our imagination, let us read it so as to see how it applies to every sort of reasonable life—and then we shall be in possession of the solution of our moral problem. Then we shall know what it is that, if we are indeed rational, we really choose to do so soon as we learn how to live.

VI

If we consider carefully any such faithful lives as I have just exemplified, we see that, however simple-minded and unreflective some of the people may be who learn to live in this way, the motives that guide them are such as will bear a great deal of thoughtful reflection.

The people whom I have in mind, and of whom such instances teach us something, are, in the first place, individuals of considerable wealth and strength of personal character. They certainly are resolute. They have a will of their own. They make choices. And so the contribution of their individual experience to their moral purpose is large. It would be wrong to say, as some do, that they are characterised by mere "altruism," by utter "self-forgetfulness," by "living solely for others." If you were on a wreck in a storm, and the lighthouse keeper were coming out to save you, you would take little comfort in the belief, if you had such a belief, that, since he was a man who had always "lived for others," he had never allowed himself the selfish delight of being fond of handling a boat with skill or of swimming for the mere love of the water. No, on the contrary, you would rejoice to believe, if you could, that he had always delighted in boating and in swimming, and was justly vain of his prowess on the water. The more of a self he had delightedly or with a just pride trained on the water, the more of a self he might have to save you with. When we are in desperate need, we never wish beings who, as some say, "have no thought of self" to help us in our plight. We want robust helpers who have been trained through their personal fondness for the skill and the prowess that they can now show in helping us. So individual self-development belongs of necessity to the people whose faithfulness we are to prize in an emergency. And if people resolve to become effectively faithful in some practical service, their principle of action includes individual self-development.

In the second place, people of the type whom I here have in mind have strong social motives. Their faithfulness is a recognition of the significance, in their eyes, of some socially important call. And this, of course, is too obvious a fact to need further mention.

But in the third place, these people are guided by a motive which distinguishes their type of social consciousness from the chance and fickle interests in this or that form of personal and social success which I exemplified a short time since. A peculiar grace has been indeed granted to them—a free gift, but one which they can only accept by being ready to earn it—a precious treasure that they cannot possess without loving and serving the life that has thus endowed them—a talent which they cannot hide, but must employ to earn new usury—a talent which seems to them not to belong to themselves, but to their master, who will require it of them, increased. This grace, this gift, is what may be called their Cause. Sometimes it appears to them in winning guise, seen in the depths of the eyes of a beloved one, or symbolised by a flag, or expressed through a song. Sometimes they think of it more austerely, and name it "science," or "the service," or "the truth." Sometimes they conceive it expressly as a religious object, and call it, not unwisely, "God's will." But however they conceive it, or whatever name they give to it, it has certain features by which you may easily know it.

The Cause, for people of this spirit, is never one individual person alone, even if, as in the lover's case, the devoted person centres it about the self of one beloved. For even the lovers know that they transfigure the beloved being, and speak of their love in terms that could not be true, unless that which they really serve were much more than any one individual. The Cause for any such devoted servant of a cause as we have been describing *is some conceived, and yet also real, spiritual unity which links many individual lives in one, and which is therefore essentially superhuman, in exactly the sense in which we found the realities of the world of the reason to be superhuman.* Yet the cause is not, on that ac-

count, any mere abstraction. It is a live something:
"My home," "my family," "my country," "my service," "mankind," "the church," "my art," "my
Science," "the cause of humanity," or, once more,
"God's will,"—such are names for the cause. One
thinks of all these objects as living expressions of
what perfectly concrete and needy people want and
require. But one also thinks of the cause as unifying
many individuals in its service, and as graciously furnishing to them what they need, namely, the opportunity to be one in spirit. The cause, then, is something based upon human needs, and inclusive of
human efforts, and alive with all the warmth of human consciousness and of human love and desire and
effort. One also thinks of the cause as *superhuman
in the scope, the wealth, the unity, and the reasonableness of its purposes and of its accomplishments.*

Such is the cause. That the individual loves it
is, in any one case, due to the chances of his temperament and of his development. That it can be
conceived and served is a matter of social experience. That it is more worthy to be served than
are any passing whims, individual or social, is the
insight which the individual gets whenever he surveys his life in its wider unities. That to serve it
requires creative effort; that it cannot be served
except by positive deeds is the result of all one's
knowledge of it. That in such service one finds
self-expression even in and through self-surrender,
and is more of a self even because one gives one's

self, is the daily experience of all who have found
such a cause. That such service enables one to face
fortune with a new courage, because, whatever happens to the servant of the cause, he is seeking not
his own fortune, but that of the cause, and has
therefore discounted his own personal defeats, is
the result of the whole spirit here in question.

For such a practical attitude toward such a cause
I know no better name than the good old word
Loyalty. And hereupon we are ready for a statement of the principle which dominates loyal lives.
All the foregoing cases were cases of loyalty. In
each some one had found a cause, a live spiritual
unity, above his own individual level. This cause
is no mere heap or collection of other human beings;
it is a life of many brethren in unity. The simplest
statement of the principle of the loyal person was
the maxim: "*Be loyal to your cause.*" Somewhat
more fully stated this principle would read: "*Devote your whole self to your cause.*" Such a principle
does not mean "Lose yourself," or "Abolish yourself," or even simply "Sacrifice yourself." It
means: "Be as rich and full and strong a self as
you can, and then, with all your heart and your soul
and your mind and your strength, devote yourself
to this your cause, to this spiritual unity in which
individuals may be, and (when they are loyal) actually are, united in a life whose meaning is above
the separate meanings of any or of all natural human beings."

Yet even thus the principle which actually inspires every thoroughly loyal action has not been fully stated. For, as we have seen, the warriors, despite the fact that their duty requires them to compass if they can the defeat of their foes, best show their loyal spirit if they prize the loyalty of their foes and honour loyalty wherever they find it. We call such a spirit that honours loyalty in the foe a spirit of chivalry. You and I may remember that Lee was the foe of that Union in whose triumph we now rejoice. Yet we may and should look upon him as, in his own personal intent, a model of the spirit of true loyalty; for he gave all that he had and was to what he found to be his cause. Such an insight into the meaning of the loyalty of the foe, chivalry requires. Therefore, the true spirit of loyalty, including, as is reasonable, this spirit of chivalry, also requires us to state the principle of loyalty in a still deeper and more universal form. The true principle of loyalty is, in fact, an union of two principles. The first is: *Be loyal.* The second is: *So be loyal, that is, so seek, so accept, so serve your cause that thereby the loyalty of all your brethren throughout all the world, through your example, through your influence, through your own love of loyalty wherever you find it, as well as through the sort of loyalty which you exemplify in your deeds, shall be aided, furthered, increased so far as in you lies.*

Can this principle be acted out? Can it direct life? Is it a barren abstraction? Let the life and the deed of the lonely lighthouse keeper give the reply. Who, amongst us, whatever his own cause, is not instructed and aided in his loyalty by the faithful deed of such a devoted soul? Such people are then, in truth, not loyal *merely* to their own private cause. *They are loyal to the cause of all loyal people.* For, to any enlightened survey of life, all the loyal, even when chance and human blindness force them at any moment to war with one another, are, in fact, spiritual brethren. They have a common cause—the cause of furthering universal loyalty through their own choice and their own service. The spirit of chivalry simply brings this fact to mind. The loyal are inspired by the loyal, are sustained by them. Every one of them finds in the loyal his kindred, his fellow-servants. Whoever is concretely loyal, that is, whoever wholly gives himself to some cause that binds many human souls in one superhuman unity, is just in so far serving the cause not only of all mankind, but of all the rational spiritual world. I repeat then: The true principle of all the loyal is: *So be loyal to your own cause as thereby to serve the advancement of the cause of universal loyalty.*

Now of the principle thus formulated I assert that it is a principle fit to be made the basis of an universal moral code. There is no duty, there is no virtue whose warrant and whose value you cannot deduce from this one principle. Charity, justice, fidelity, decisiveness, strenuousness, truthfulness, efficiency, wise self-assertion, watchful self-restraint, patience, defiance of fortune, resignation in defeat, your daily social duties, your individual self-development, your personal rights and dignity, your obedience to the calls of duty, your justified self-sacrifices, your rational pride in the unique moral office to which you have individually been called—all these, I assert, can be rightly defined, defended, estimated, and put into practice through an accurate understanding and development of the principle of loyalty just laid down.

Since I am, indeed, speaking of sources of insight, and am not portraying at any length their results, you will not expect of me a deduction of such a moral code here. But this assertion of mine is no mere boast. I have repeatedly endeavoured, elsewhere, to portray loyalty and to apply its principles to life. For the moment it suffices to ask you to consider the lives of the loyal, in such examples as I have suggested to you, and to try for yourselves to see what they teach. To help you in such a consideration, I may here simply remind you that when one is not only loyal but enlightened, one cannot finally approve or accept any cause or any mode of living that, while seeming in itself to be a cause or a mode of living such as embodies the spirit of loyalty, still depends upon or involves contempt for the loyalty of other men, or a disposition to prey upon their loyalty and to deprive them of any cause to which they can be loyal. No loyalty that lives by destroying the loyalty of your neighbour is just to its own true intent. And that is why charity and justice are fruits of the loyal spirit. And that is why, if your cause and your loyal action are rightly accepted and carried out, the common interests of all rational beings are served by your loyalty precisely in so far as your powers permit. Whatever your special cause (and your special personal cause —your love, your home, or your calling—you must have), *your true cause is the spiritual unity of all the world of reasonable beings.* This cause you further, so far as in you lies, by your every deed.

And that also is why the principle of loyalty, once rightly defined and served by you—served with the whole energy and power of your personal self—is a principle that, upon any enlightened survey of your life you can never regret having served. This, then, is what we were seeking—an absolute moral principle, a guide for all action.

But even this is not the whole meaning of what the spirit of loyalty has to teach you. Your cause, thus concretely and yet universally defined, is something of which you can always, and now truthfully and without any pathetic fallacy, say, what Browning's lover said in the lyric that I quoted in our second lecture:

> " World, how it walled about
>   Life with disgrace,
> Till God's own smile came out
>   That was thy face."

For your cause can only be revealed to you through some presence that first teaches you to love this unity of the spiritual life. This presence will come to you in a beloved form, as something human, dear, vitally fascinating. It may be a person—a face— or a living community of human beings that first reveals it to you. You can, indeed, choose it as your cause. Your will is needed. Loyalty is no mere sentiment. It is the willing and practical and thorough-going devotion of a self to a cause. But you can never choose your cause until you have first found it. And you must find it in human shape. And you must love it before you can choose its service.

Therefore, however far you go in loyalty, you will never regard your loyalty as a mere morality. It will also be in essence a religion. It will always be to you a finding of an object that comes to you from without and above, as divine grace has always been said to come. Hence loyalty is a source not only of moral but of religious insight. The spirit of true loyalty is of its very essence a complete synthesis of the moral and of the religious interests. The cause is a religious object. It finds you in your need. It points out to you the way of salvation. Its presence in your world is to you a free gift from the realm of the spirit—a gift that you have not of yourself, but through the willingness of the world to manifest to you the way of salvation. This free gift first compels your love. Then you freely give yourself in return.

Therefore, the spirit of loyalty completely reconciles those bitter and tragic wrangles between the mere moralists and the partisans of divine grace. It supplies in its unity also the way to define, in harmonious fashion, the ideal of what your individual experience seeks in its need, of what your social world, groaning and travailing in pain together, longs for as our common salvation, of what the reason conceives as the divine unity of the world's meaning, of what the rational will requires you to serve as God's will. Through loyalty, then, not only the absolute moral insight, but the absolute religious insight, as you grow in grace and persist in service, may be and will be gradually and truthfully revealed to you.

For loyalty, though justifying no "moral holidays," shows you the will of the spiritual world, the divine will, and so gives you rest in toil, peace in the midst of care. And loyalty also, though leaving you in no mystic trance, displays to you the law that holds the whole rational world together; though showing you the divine grace, calls upon you for the strenuous giving of your whole self to action; though requiring of you no philosophical training, tells you what the highest reason can but justify; and, though concerned with no mere signs and wonders, shows you the gracious and eternal miracle of a spiritual realm where, whatever fortunes and miracles and divine beings there may be, you, in so far as you are loyal, are and are to be always at home.

And all this is true because the spirit of loyalty
at once expresses your own personal need and reason, and defines for you the only purpose that could
be justified from the point of view of one who surveyed all voluntary and rational life. This is the
purpose to further the unity of whatever spiritual
life you can influence, and to do this by your every
rational deed, precisely in so far as your powers permit. This is a law for all rational beings. No
angels could do more than this.

There is a famous word that Chaucer put into the
mouth of his Griselda at the moment when her husband tried her patience with his last and utmost
cruelty. That word, uttered by a woman to a mere
individual human creature who happened to be her
husband, seems helplessly pathetic and slavish
enough. Yet Chaucer himself warns us that the
old tale, truly interpreted, should be viewed as an
allegory of the deeper relations between the soul
and God. Even so, to many of our leading modern
minds the allegory, when interpreted in this way,
may seem harsh enough. Mere moralists may make
light of it, because it seems opposed to the dignity
of the moral spirit of individual self-respect. Only
the partisans of a divine grace, administered through
inscrutable divine decrees, would, you might suppose, still see any worth in so cruel an allegory.
Nevertheless, this judgment of the allegory is false.
Let a truly loyal being—our lighthouse keeper, for
instance—our patriot or martyr, let Lee or Newton,

let whoever is filled with the right spirit of loyalty—
whoever, through the light that he trims, intends to
lighten and to unify so much of the spiritual world
as he can ever reach by his deed—let *such* a loyal
being utter Griselda's word. Let him utter it as
in the presence of the master of life, who offers to
all the loyal the divine grace of finding themselves
through their devotion to their cause. Let him
address this word

> "As unto one that hears
> A cry above the conquered years."

Let him utter this word as the summary and confession of his whole life of loyalty. And then Griselda's word is no longer slavish. It is full of the
resolute courage, of the splendid contempt for mere
fortune, of the unconquerable spiritual self-assertion, yes, it is full of the deathless will, which are
of the very essence of loyalty, and which, indeed,
must overcome and, in the eternal realm, do overcome the world.

Griselda's word was this:

> "But certes, Lord, for none adversitie,
> To dien in this case it shall not be
> That I in herte and minde should aye repente,
> That I you gave my soul with whole intente."

Whoever thus addresses his word, not to a human
individual, but as unto the master of life, and then,

sincerely and persistently and lovingly, lives that word out in his life, has solved the religious paradox. From out the lonely and darkened depths of his personal finitude, from out the chaos of his social promptings and of his worldly ambitions, amid all the storms of fortune, "midst of hell's laughter and noises appalling," he has heard the voice of the Spirit. He has heard, and—however unlearned— he has understood. His own lamp is burning, and through his deed the eternal light shines in the darkness of this world.

VI

THE RELIGIOUS MISSION OF SORROW

VI

THE RELIGIOUS MISSION OF SORROW

It very often happens to us that to reach any notable result, either in life or in insight, is even thereby to introduce ourselves to a new problem. In the present state of the undertaking of these lectures such is our experience. The religious insight whose source is the loyal spirit was our topic in the foregoing lecture. If my own view is correct, this source is by far the most important that we have yet considered. It unites the spirit and the meaning of all the foregoing sources. Rightly interpreted, it points the way to a true salvation.

Yet the very last words of our sketch of the fruits of loyalty were of necessity grave words. Intending to show through what spirit man escapes from total failure, we were brought face to face with the tragedies which still beset the higher life. "Adversity"—poor Griselda faced it in the tale. We left the loyal spirit appearing to us—as it does appear in its strongest representatives, able, somehow, in the power that is due to its insight, to triumph over fortune. But side by side with this suggestion of the nature of that which overcomes the world stood the inevitable reminder of the word: "In this world ye shall have tribulation."

How is tribulation related to religious insight? That is our present problem. It has been forced upon our attention by the study of the place and the meaning of loyalty. Some understanding of this problem is necessary to any further comprehension of the lessons of all the foregoing sources of insight, and is of peculiar significance for any definition of the office of religion.

To nearly all of us, at some time in our lives, and to many of us at all times, the tragic aspect of human life seems to be a profound hindrance to religious insight of any stable sort. I must here first bring more fully to your minds why this is so—why the existence of tragedy in human existence appears to many moods, and to many people, destructive of faith in any religious truth and a barrier against rational assurance regarding the ultimate triumph of anything good. Then I want to devote the rest of this lecture to showing how sorrow, how the whole burden of human tribulation, has been, and reasonably may be, not merely a barrier in the way of insight, but also a source of religious insight. And this is the explanation of the title of the present lecture.

I

We approach our problem fully mindful of the limitations to which the purpose of these lectures confines us. The problem of evil has many metaphysical, theological, moral, and common-sense aspects upon which I can say nothing whatever in the present context. Human sorrow appears in our pathway in these lectures as a topic for us to consider, first, because whatever source of religious insight we have thus far consulted has shown us man struggling with some sort of ill, and, secondly, because there are aspects of this very struggle which will provide us with a new source of religious insight, and which will thus tend to throw new light upon the meaning of all the other sources. A thorough-going study of the problem of evil would require of us a complete philosophy not only of religion but of reality. But we are limiting ourselves, in these discussions, to a survey of certain sources.

The reasons why the existence and the prominence of evil in human life seem to all of us at some times, and to many of us at all times, a hindrance to the acceptance of any religious solution of the problems of life are familiar. I need then only to remind you what they are.

Without going into any subtleties regarding the definition of evil, it is obvious that our first characteristic reaction when we meet with what we take to be an evil is an effort to get rid of it, to shun its presence, or to remove it from existence. Pain, cold, burning heat, disease, starvation, death, our enemies, our dangers, these are facts that, precisely so far as we find them evil, we face with the determination to annul altogether their evil aspect.

A characteristic result of this tendency appears in the fact that man, who of all animals is most clearly aware of the presence of evil in his world, is for that very reason not only an ingenious deviser of new inventions for getting good things and for supplying his needs, but is also the most destructive of animals. He wars with his natural surroundings, and still more with his fellow-men, in ways that show how the instinctive aversions upon which his estimates of evil are founded are reinforced by the habits which he forms in his contests with ill fortune. Man the destroyer of evil thus appears, in much of his life, as a destroyer who is also largely moved by a love of destruction for its own sake. This love plays a great part in the formation of even very high levels of our social and moral consciousness. The heroes of song and story, and often of history as well, are fascinating partly, or chiefly, because they could kill and did so. We love victory over ill. Killing seems to involve such a victory. So we love killing, at least in the hero tales. The result is often a certain inconsistency. The gods offered Achilles the choice between a short life full of the glorious slaying of enemies and a long life of harmless obscurity. He chose the short life; and therefore he is to be remembered forever. For even when he would not fight, his "destructive wrath sent the souls of many valiant heroes to Hades, and left themselves a prey to the dogs and birds of the air." And when he returned to battle, what became of Hector? The song of the Nibelungs opens by assuring us that the old stories tell of many wonders, and of heroes worthy of praise (*von Helden lobebaeren*), and of great labours (*von grosser Arebeit*). These "great labours" consisted mainly in the slaying of other men. And this slaying was obviously "worthy of praise"; for it gave us a model for all our own struggle with evil. As for the heroes of history, of course, we love to dwell upon their constructive labours. But, after all, what sort of comparison is there in what the plain man, apart from a higher enlightenment, usually calls glory, between Washington and Napoleon? No doubt there will always be admirers of Napoleon who will think of him as a misunderstood reformer labouring for the building up of an ideal Europe. But even such admirers will join with the plain man in dwelling, with especial fascination, upon the Napoleon of Austerlitz. And they will not forget even Borodino. No doubt the lovers of Washington find him glorious. But where, in his career, belongs the glory of having put an end to the Holy Roman Empire, or of having destroyed the polity of the Europe of the old maps?

Man the destroyer thus glories in his prowess,
and adores the heroes who were the ministers of
death. And since, of course, his warfare is always
directed against something that he takes to be an
evil, the principle which directs his glorious conflicts seems to be one easy of general statement, inconsistent as some of the reasonings founded upon
it seem to be. This principle is: "All evil ought
to be destroyed. There ought to be none. It
should be swept out of existence."

Of course, when the principle of the warfare with
evil is thus abstractly stated, it does not tell us what
we are to regard as an evil. It leaves the wise estimate of good and evil to be learned through a
closer study of the facts of life. No doubt, then,
Achilles, and the other heroes of song and story,
may have become as glorious as they are by reason
of our excessive love of destruction due to some
imperfect estimate of the true values of life. And
therefore the mere statement of the principle leaves
open a very wide range for difference of opinion and
for inconsistency of view as to what it is that ought
to be destroyed. The natural estimate of the plain
man, when he loves the heroes of old, seems to imply
that one of the chief ills that man ought to destroy
usually takes the form of some other man. And
this way of estimating men in terms of their success in killing other men has its obvious inconsis-
tencies. But, after all, as one may insist, much is
gained when we have made up our minds as to what

ought to be done with evil, whether evil is incorporated in our enemies, in our pains, or in our sins. We may leave to advancing civilisation, or perhaps to some triumph of religion, the correction of our excessive fondness for the destruction of human life. What is essentially important is that it is part of man's mission to destroy evil. And about this general teaching the saints and the warriors, so it seems, may well agree.

Religion, it may be said, can have nothing to urge against this fundamental axiom. So far all appears clear. Evil ought to be driven out of the world. Common-sense says this. Every struggle with climate or with disease or with our foes is carried on in this spirit. The search for salvation is itself—so one may insist—simply another instance of this destructive conflict with impending ills. All that is most elemental in our hatreds thus agrees with whatever is loftiest in our souls, in facing evils with our "everlasting No." All the differences of moral opinion are mere differences as to what to destroy. Man is always the destroyer of ill.

II

But if you grant the general principle thus stated, the presence of evil in this world, in the forms that we all recognise, and in the degree of importance that it attains in all our lives, seems, indeed, a very serious hindrance in the way of religious insight.

And the reason is plain.   Religion, as we have said, in seeking salvation, seeks some form of communion with the master of life.   That is, it seeks to come into touch with a power, a principle, or a mind, or a heart, that, on the one hand, possesses, or, with approval, surveys or controls the real nature of things, and that, on the other hand, welcomes us in our conflicts with evil, supports our efforts, and secures our success.   I have made no effort, in these lectures, to define a theological creed.   Such a creed forms a topic in which I take great interest but which lies beyond the limitations of this discourse. Yet our study of the historical relations between religion and morality, our earlier analysis of the religious need, have shown us that unless you are able to make some sort of effective appeal to principles that link you with the whole nature of things, your religious need must remain unsatisfied, and your last word will have to take, at best, the form of a moral, not a religious doctrine.   Religion does not require us to solve all mysteries; but it does require for its stability some assurance that, so far as concerns our need of salvation, and despite the dangers that imperil our salvation, those that are with us, when we are rightly enlightened, are more than those that are against us.

In order to make this fact yet clearer, let us suppose that all such assurance is taken away from us. Review the result.   Let it be supposed that we need salvation.   Let it be granted that, as we naturally

are, in our blindness and narrowness, and in the caprices of our passions, we cannot find the way out
unless we can get into touch with some spiritual
unity and reasonable life such as the loyal man's
cause seems to reveal to him. Let it be further
supposed, however, that all human causes are, in
their way and time, as much subject to chance and
to the capricious blows of fortune as we ourselves
individually are. Let it be imagined that the cause
of causes, the unity of the whole spiritual world, is,
in fact, a mere dream. Let the insight of the reason
and of the will, which, when taken in their unity,
have been said by me to reveal to us that the universe is in its essence Spirit, and that the cause of
the loyal is not only a reality, but *the* reality—let
this insight, I say, be regarded as an illusion. Let
no other spiritual view of reality prove probable.
Then, indeed, we shall be left merely with ideals of
life in our hands, but with no assurance that real
life, in its wholeness, approves or furthers these
ideals. Our need of salvation will then, to be sure,
still remain. Our definition of what salvation would
be if it should become ours will be unchanged. But,
having thus abandoned as illusory or as uncertain
all the sources of insight which I have so far been
defending, we shall have upon our hands only the
moral struggle for the good as our best resource.
We shall then hope for no assurance of salvation.
We shall abandon religion to the realm of mythical
consolations, and shall face a grim world with only

such moral courage as we can muster for the uncertain conflict.   Our loyalty itself will lose its religious aspect.   For the objective goodness of our cause—the divine grace which its presence seems to offer to our life—will no longer mean anything but a faint and uncertain hope, which we shall keep or not according to the caprices of our personal resolutions. Such, I say, would be the outcome of rejecting all sources of religious insight into the real nature of things.

The result, in the case now supposed, will be one which any honest man will indeed accept if he must, but which no one can regard as including any satisfactory religious insight whatever.   I certainly do not here present these considerations as in themselves any arguments for religion, or as in themselves furnishing support for our previous arguments regarding the nature and the merits of the sources of insight which we have been reviewing.   The case for which I have argued in the foregoing lectures must indeed stand or fall solely upon its own merits. And if the reason and the will, as the spirit of loyalty interprets and unifies their teachings, do *not* really show us any truth about the whole nature of things, I would not for a moment ask to have their teachings tolerated merely because, without such teachings, we should lose our grounds for holding to a religious interpretation of life.   If we *must* fall back upon mere moral resoluteness, and abandon any assurance as to the religious objects, and as to the way and the attainment of salvation, I, for one, am quite ready to accept the call of life, and to fight on for a good end so long as I can, without seeking for religious consolations that have once been shown to be mythical. But I have indicated to you, in general, my grounds for holding that our previous sources actually *do* give us an insight which is not only moral but religious, and *do* throw light upon our relations to a reason which moves in all things, to a divine will which expresses itself in all the universe, and to a genuine revelation of its purposes which this makes of itself when it inspires our loyalty. My present purpose is, not to reinforce these grounds by the mere threat that their rejection would involve an abandonment of any well-grounded religious assurance, but to present to you the fact that religion is, indeed, a search for a really divine foundation for the saving process.

Religion differs from morality in looking beyond our own active resoluteness for something—not ourselves—that gives a warrant, founded in the whole nature of things—a warrant for holding that this resoluteness will succeed and will bring us into union with that which saves.

Hence it is, indeed, true that if there is *no* master of life with whom we can come into touch, *no* triumph of the good in the universe, *no* real source of salvation—religion must result in disappointment. And then our only recourse must, indeed, be the moral will. This recourse is one that, as we have seen, many in our time are quite ready to accept. And such, in my own opinion, are for reasons that they do not themselves admit actually well on their way toward real salvation. Only it is useless to attribute to them, in their present stage of conviction, any conscious and assured possession of religious insight. To sum up, then, religion demands the presence of the master of life as a real being, and depends upon holding that the good triumphs.

But if we attempt to combine the two assertions, "All evil ought to be destroyed" and "In the universe as a whole the good triumphs," and hereupon to face the facts of human life as religion finds them, we are at once involved in familiar perplexities. With many of these perplexities the limitations of the present discussion, as already explained, forbid us to deal. I am merely trying to show, for the moment, why the presence of evil in our lives seems to be a hindrance in the way of religious insight. And it is enough if I emphasise at this point what must readily come to the consciousness of all of you when you consider the situation in which our whole argument seems now to have placed us.

The very existence of the religious need itself presupposes not only the presence, but the usual prevalence of very great evils in human life. For unless man is in great danger of missing the pearl of great price, he stands in no need of a saving process. A religious man may come to possess an acquired optimism—the hard-won result of the religious process which seems to him to have pointed out the way of salvation. But a man who begins with the assurance that all is ordinarily well with human nature is precluded from religion, in our sense of the word religion, by his very type of optimism. Such an optimist of the "first intention," such a believer that in the main it is well with human nature, can be, as we have seen, a moralist, although he is usually a very simple-minded moralist, as unaware of the graver moral problems as he is cheerfully indifferent to the hard case in which most of his brethren live. But whoever sees the deep need of human salvation, as the various cynics and rebels and sages and prophets whom we cited in our first lecture have seen it, has begun by recognising the bitterness of human loss and defeat—the gravity of the evil case of the natural man. Were not the world as it now is very evil, what, then, were the call for religion? Religion takes its origin in our sense of deep need —in other words, in our recognition that evil has a very real place in life. "*Tempora pessima*"— "The times are very evil"—is thus no phrase of a merely mediæval type of world-hatred. The woes of man are the presupposed basis of fact upon which the search for salvation rests.

And the further one goes in the pursuit of the sources of religious insight, the more, as we have ourselves found, does one's original recognition of the ill of the human world become both deepened and varied. From the solitude of one's individual sorrows one goes out to seek for religious relief in the social world, only to find how much more manifold the chaos of ordinary social life is than is the conflict of one's private passions. If one asks guidance from reason, reason appears at first as a sort of spirit brooding upon the face of the depths of unreason. When loyalty itself is created, it finds itself beset by adversities. If evil drives us to seek relief in religion, religion thus teaches us to know, better and better, the tragedy of life. Its first word is, thus, about evil and about the escape from evil. But its later words appear to have been a persistent discourse upon our tribulations.

But how can religion, thus presupposing the presence of evil in our life, and illustrating this presence anew at every step, undertake to lead us to any assurance of the triumph of a good principle in the real world, in case, as seems so far obvious, such a triumph of a good principle would mean that all evil is to be simply destroyed and wiped out of existence?

Briefly restating the situation, it is this: If the evils of human life are indeed but transient and superficial incidents, or if—to use a well-known extreme form of statement—evil is an "unreality" altogether—then religion is superfluous. For there is no need of salvation unless man's ordinary case is, indeed, very really a hard case, that is, unless evil is a reality, and a deep-rooted one. But, on the other hand, if evil is thus deep-rooted in the very conditions of human life as they are, and if it persists upon higher levels even of the religious life, religion seems in danger of total failure. For unless goodness is somehow at the real heart of things—is, so to speak, the core of reality—the hope of salvation is a dream, and religion deceives us. But goodness, by the hypothesis that we are just now considering, requires that evil should be wholly abolished. How can that which should not exist at all, namely, evil, be in such wise the expression of the real nature of things that on the one hand religion is needed to save us from evil, and yet is able to do so only by bringing us to know that the real nature of things is good? Here is our problem. And it is a hard one.

In brief, as you may say, religion must take its choice. Either the evil in the world is of no great importance, and then religion is useless; or the need of salvation is great, and the way is straight and narrow; and then evil is deeply rooted in the very nature of reality, and religion seems a failure.

III

I believe that there is some advantage in stating in this somewhat crabbed and dialectical fashion, a problem which most of us usually approach through much more direct and pathetic experience. One advantage in crabbedness and in fondness for dialectic is that it sometimes tends to clear away the clouds

with which emotion from moment to moment sur-
rounds certain great problems of life. As I said
earlier, in speaking of the office of the reason, abstract ideas are but means to an end. Their end
is to help us to a clear and rational survey of the
connections of things. When you are to examine the
landscape from a height, in order to obtain a wide
prospect, you may have to use a glass, or a compass, or some other instrument of abstraction, in
order to define what the distance tends to render
obscure, or what the manifoldness of the scenery
surveyed makes it hard rightly to view in its true
relations. And, in such cases, the glass or the compass is but an auxiliary, intended to help in the
end your whole outlook. Now the world of good
and evil is a world of wide prospects, of vast dis-
tances, of manifold features. A bit of dialectics,
using abstract and one-sided considerations in succession, may prepare the way for seeing the whole
better.

The plain man well knows the problem that I
have just been characterising. He knows how it
may enter his religious life. Only he does not usually think of it abstractly. It pierces his heart.
Stunned by a grief, he may say: "I have trusted
God, and now he forsakes me. How can a good
God permit this horror in my life?" Yet the plain
man, if religiously minded, also knows what is meant
by saying, "Out of the depths have I cried." And
he knows, too, that part of the preciousness of his

very idea of God depends upon the fact that there
are depths, and that out of them one *can* cry, and
that God is precisely a 'being who somehow hears
the cry from the depths. God, "pragmatically viewed," as some of our recent teachers express the matter, is thus often defined for the plain man's religious
experience as a helper in trouble. Were there no
trouble, there would be, then, it would seem, no
cry of the soul for such a being, and very possibly
no such being conceived by the soul that now cries.
Yet this very God—one cries to him because he is
supposed to be all-powerful, and to do all things
well, and therefore to be a very present help in
time of trouble. All this seems clear enough at the
time when one is on the way up, out of the depths,
or when one begins to praise God in the Psalm-
ist's words, because, as one now says: "He hath
planted my feet upon a rock, and hath established
my goings." But how does all this seem at the
moment when one suddenly falls into the pit of
sorrow, and when one's eyes are turned downward;
when he who doeth all things well permits the utmost treachery of fortune, and when the one who
can hear every cry seems deaf to one's most heart-
rending pleadings? The familiar explanation that all
this is a penalty for one's sins may awaken an echo
of Job's protest in the mind of the man who knows
not how he has deserved this woe, or may arouse the
deeper and now consciously dialectical comments
on the mystery involved in the fact that God per-

mits sin. "Why was I made thus blind and sinful?" one may cry. And hereupon religious insight becomes, indeed, confused enough, and may turn for relief to that well-known type of defiance which, if not religious, is at least moral; for it is a protest against evil. If at such moments God is, indeed, to our darkened vision, and, for us, who wait for his blessing, as if he were sleeping or on a journey, one can at least, as moral agent, utter this protest against ill, and wonder why his omnipotence does not make it effective. One thus begins, as it were, to try heroically to do the absent God's work for him.

All these are familiar experiences. They find us, too often, unprepared. They find us when emotion tends to cloud every insight. They illustrate a certain dialectical process which belongs to all human life and which plays its part in the whole history of religion. Perhaps it is well to state an aspect of this dialectical process abstractly, crabbedly, and unemotionally, as we have just done, in order that we may make ourselves the more ready to face the issue when life exemplifies it with crushing suddenness, and when

> "The painful ploughshare of passion
> Grinds down to our uttermost rock."

The problem, as just abstractly stated, is this. Religion seems to face this dilemma: Either there are no great and essential ills about human life;

and then there is no great danger of perdition, and
no great need of salvation, and religion has no
notable office; or there are great and essential ills,
and man's life is in bitter need of salvation; but in
that case evil is deeply rooted in the very nature
of the reality from which we have sprung; and
therefore religion has no right to assure us of communion with a real master of life who is able to do
with evil what not only ought to be done with it,
but ought always to have been done with it by any
being able to offer man any genuine salvation. For
(as we are assuming) what ought to be done, yes,
what ought to have been done with evil from the
beginning, is and was this: To banish it altogether
from existence.

This, I say, is, when abstractly stated, the
dilemma in which religion seems to be placed. Of
this dilemma the countless struggles of the human
soul when, in the spirit of some practical religion,
it seeks for salvation and faces its woes are examples. These struggles are infinitely pathetic and
in life are often confusing to insight. Is there any
value in considering this abstract statement of the
principles upon which this dilemma seems to be
founded? Possibly there is, if we can hereby be
led also to consider—not indeed, in this place, the
problems of theology, or the metaphysics of evil,
but a new source of insight.

IV

This new source of insight begins to come to us when we observe, as we can often observe if we listen with closer attention to the voices of our own hearts, that the general principle, "Evil ought simply to be put out of existence," does *not* express our whole attitude toward all evils, and gives only an imperfect account either of our more commonplace and elemental or of our more elevated, heroic, and reasonable estimates of life.

The principle: "Evil ought to be simply abolished," is, indeed, one that we unquestionably apply, in our ordinary life, to a vast range of natural ills. But it is not universal. Let us first indicate its apparent range. Physical pain, when sufficiently violent, is an example of an ill that appears to us, in all its greater manifestations, plainly intolerable. So it seems to us to illustrate the principle that "Evil ought to be put out of existence." We desire, with regard to it, simply its abolition. The same is true of what one may call *unassimilated* griefs of all levels—the shocks of calamity at the moment when they first strike, the anguish of loss or of disappointment precisely when these things are new to us and appear to have no place in our life-plan. These are typical ills. And they all illustrate ills that seem to us to be worthy only of destruction. The magnitude of such ills as factors in

the individual and in the social world often appears
to us immeasurable. Pestilence, famine, the cruel-
ties of oppressors, the wrecks of innocent human
lives by cruel fortunes—all these seem, for our ordinary estimates, facts that we can in no wise assimilate, justify, or reasonably comprehend. That
is, we can see, in the single case, no reason why such
events should form part of human life—except that
so it indeed is. They seem, to our natural understanding, simply opaque data of experience, to be
annulled or removed if we can. And to such ills,
from our human point of view, the principle: "They
ought to be simply driven out of existence," is naturally applied without limitation. The apparent
range of this principle is therefore, indeed, very
wide.

Now it forms no part of our present discourse to
consider in detail the possible theological or metaphysical basis for a possible explanation of such ills.
I have elsewhere written too much and too often
about the problem of evil to be subject to the accu-
sation of neglecting the pathos and the tragedy of
these massive ills. This, however, I can at once
say. *In so far as* ills appear to us thus, they are,
indeed, *no* sources of religious insight. On the
other hand, even when thus viewed, in all their
blackness, they can be, and are, sources of moral
enthusiasm and earnestness. Man the destroyer,
when, awaking to the presence of such ills in his
world, he contends with them, gets a perfectly defi-

nite moral content into his life. And he has his
right to do so. Whatever his religion, he is morally
authorised to labour against these unmediated evils
with the heartiest intolerance. When such labour
takes on social forms, it helps toward the loftiest
humanity. The war with pain and disease and
oppression, the effort to bind up wounds and to
snatch souls from destruction—all these things constitute some of man's greatest opportunities for loyalty. Nevertheless, when man loyally wars with
the ills such as physical anguish and pestilence and
famine and oppression, he does *not* thereby tend to
discover, through his own loyal act, why such individual ills are permitted in the world. In so far
as these evils give him opportunity for service, they
appeal to his loyalty as a warrior against them. If
his cause includes, for him, activities that enter into
this warfare with ills that are to be destroyed, these
ills have thus indirectly conduced to his religious
life. But it is his loyalty that in such cases is his
source of religious insight. The ills themselves that
he thus destructively fights remain to him as opaque
as before. Why they find their place in the world
he does not see. Now that they are found there,
he knows what to do with them—namely, to annul
them, to put them out of existence, as a part of his
loyal service. But if he is religiously minded, he
does not for a moment conceive that the ills with
which he wars are there simply to give him the opportunity for his service. So far then it is, indeed,

true that the ills which we have simply to destroy offer us no source of religious insight.

But now, as I must insist, *not all* the ills that we know are of this nature. Wide and deep and terrible as are those conflicts with the incomprehensible ills of fortune whose presence in the world we do not understand, there are other ills. And toward these other ills we take an attitude which is not wholly destructive. We find them, upon a closer view, inseparably bound up with good—so closely bound up therewith that we could not conceive a life wherein this sort of good which is here bound up with this sort of ill could be separated therefrom. In these cases the principle: "Evil should be simply put out of existence," proves to be a palpable falsity. As our knowledge of such ills grows clearer, we commonly find that there is, indeed, something about them, as they at any one moment appear to us, which ought, indeed, to be annulled, set aside, destroyed. But this annulling of one momentary or at least transient aspect of the ill is but part, in such cases, of a constructive process, which involves growth rather than destruction—a passage to a new life rather than a casting wholly out of life. Such ills we remove only in so far as we assimilate them, idealise them, take them up into the plan of our lives, give them meaning, set them in their place in the whole.

Now such ills, as I must insist, play a very great part in life and especially in the higher life. Our attitude toward them constitutes, above all, on the very highest levels of our reasonableness, a very great part of our attitude toward the whole problem of life. In the presence of these idealised evils, man the destroyer becomes transformed into man the creator. And he does so without in the least abandoning his justified moral distinctions, without indulging in any sort of "moral holiday," and without becoming unwilling to destroy when he cannot otherwise rationally face the facts before him than by destroying. He is not less strenuous in his dealing with his moral situation because he has discovered how to substitute growth for destruction and creative assimilation for barren hostility. He is all the more effectively loyal in the presence of such ills, because he sees how they can become, for his consciousness, parts of a good whole.

Ills of this sort may become, and in the better cases do become, sources of religious insight. Their presence in our world enables us the better to comprehend its spiritual unity. And because they are often very deep and tragic ills, which we face only with very deep and dear travail of spirit, they hint to us how, from the point of view of a world-embracing insight, the countless and terrible ills of the other sort, which we *cannot* now understand, and which, at present, appear to us merely as worthy of utter destruction, may still also have their places, as stages and phases of expression, in the larger life to which we belong. In our own power to assimilate and spiritualise our own ills, we can get at times a hint of such larger spiritual processes. In these very processes we also, through our loyal endeavour, can act our own real part; although *what* the larger processes are we cannot expect at present to comprehend better than a sympathising dog, whose master is devoting his life to furthering the highest spiritual welfare of a nation or of all mankind, can know why his master's face is now grief-stricken and now joyous.

In other words, the ills that we *can* spiritualise and idealise without merely destroying them hint to us that, despite the uncomprehended chaos of seemingly hopeless tragedy with which for our present view human life seems to be beset, the vision of the spiritual triumph of the good which reason and loyalty present to us need not be an illusion, but is perfectly consistent with the facts. The world is infinite. With our present view we could not expect to grasp directly the unity of its meaning. We have sources of insight which tend to our salvation by showing us, in general, although certainly not in detail, the nature of the spiritual process which, as these sources of insight persistently point out, constitutes the essence of reality. Whether these sources are themselves valid and trustworthy is a question to be considered upon its own merits. I have stated my case so far as our brief review requires it to be stated. I must leave to your own considerateness the further estimate of what these

sources teach, both as to the reality of the master
of life and as to the nature of the process of salvation.   My present concern is simply with the cloud
that the presence of evil seems to cause to pass over
the face of all these sources.   I cannot undertake
wholly to dispel this cloud by showing you in detail why pestilences or why broken hearts are permitted to exist in this world.   But I can show you
that there are, indeed, ills, and very dark ills in life,
which not only are there, but are essential to the
highest life.   I do not exaggerate our power to solve
mysteries when I insist that *these* ills constitute not
an opaque hindrance to insight, not a cloud over
the sun of reason and of loyalty, but rather a source
of insight.   And, as I insist, they constitute such a
source without being in the least an excuse for any
indolence in our moral struggle with precisely those
aspects of such ills as we ought to destroy.   They
show us how the triumph of the moral will over such
adversities is perfectly consistent with the recognition that the most rational type of life demands the
existence of just such adversities.   Their presence in
our world does not excuse sloth, does not justify
a "moral holiday," does not permit us to enjoy any
mere luxury of mystical contemplation of the triumph of the divine in the world, without ourselves
taking our rational and strenuous part in the actual
attainment of such triumph.   But what these forms
of ill show us is that there are accessible cases in
which if—but only if—one does the divine will—one

can know of the doctrine that teaches how the divine will can and does become perfect, not through the mere abolition of evil, but through suffering. Such cases of ill are true sources of insight. They reveal to us some of the deepest truths about what loyalty, and spiritual triumph, and the good really are. They make for salvation. They drive away clouds and bring us face to face with the will of the world.

I have so far spoken of evil in general. For the present purpose I need a name for the ills that one rationally faces only when one, through some essentially active, constructive, moral process, creatively assimilates and idealises them, and thus wins them over to be a part of good—not when one merely drives them out of existence. One name for such ills is Griselda's name: "Adversities." But I have chosen, in the title of this lecture, to use the vaguer untechnical name: Sorrow. A great physical pain, you in general cannot, at least at the moment, idealise. You then and there face it only as something intolerable, and can see no good except through its mere abolition. The same is true of any crushing blow of fortune, precisely in so far as it crushes. All such things you then and there view narrowly. Their mystery lies in the very fact that they are thus, for the moment, seen only narrowly. Hence, they are *ipso facto* hindrances to insight. But a sorrow—when you use the word you have already begun to assimilate and idealise the fact that you

call a sorrow. That you have begun to idealise
it, the very luxury of deep grief often vaguely hints,
sometimes clearly shows. For sorrows may have
already become tragically precious to you. Would
you forget your lost love, or your dead, or your
"days that are no more," even if you could? Is
mere destruction, then, your *only* tendency in the
presence of such sorrows. A closer view of your
attitude toward such sorrows shows that they are
not only clouding but revealing. They begin, they
may endlessly continue, to show you the way into
the spiritual realm and the nature of this realm.

By sorrow, then, I here mean an experience of ill
which is not wholly an experience of that which as
you then and there believe ought to be simply driven
out of existence. The insight of which sorrow is the
source, is an insight that tends to awaken within
you a new view of what the spiritual realm is. This
view is not in the least what some recent writers
have blindly proclaimed it to be—a philosopher's
artificial abstraction—a cruel effort to substitute a
"soft" doctrine of the study for a moral and humane
facing of the "hard" facts of human life. No, this
view is the soul of the teaching of all the world's
noblest and most practical guides to the most concrete living. This view faces hardness, it endures
and overcomes. Poets, prophets, martyrs, sages,
artists, the heroes of spirituality of every land and
clime, have found in it comfort, resolution, and triumph, The philosopher, at best, can report what

these have seen. And "soft," indeed, is the type of thoughtful effort which declines to follow with its ideas what all these have learned to express in their lives and in their religion.

V

Because I am here not stating for you a merely speculative doctrine concerning the place of evil in a good and rational spiritual world, I once more need, at this point, to appeal as directly as I can to life. Let me present to you, from recent literature, a noteworthy instance of the use of our present source of insight. The instance is confessedly one where no complete and determinate religious creed is defended as the result of the use of the insight in question. And an actually eternal truth about the spiritual world—a very old truth in the lore of the wise, but a deeply needed truth for our own day—is illustrated by the instance which the tale portrays.

I refer to a recent short story, published in the *Atlantic Monthly* for November, 1910, and written by Cornelia A. P. Comer. It is entitled "The Preliminaries." It is, to my mind, an impressive union of a genuinely effective realism and a deep symbolism. The characters are very real human beings. Their problem is one of the most familiar problems of daily life—the problem as to the advisability of the proposed marriage of two young lovers. The conditions of the problem are hard facts, of a general type that is unfortunately frequent enough under our confusing modern conditions. These facts are viewed in the tale as such people might well view them. And yet the issues involved are, like all the problems of young lovers, issues that are bound up with all the interests of religion and with the whole problem of the reality of a spiritual world. These issues are treated as they truly are, with a result that is fairly supernatural in its ancient but always new appeal to a source of insight that we can reach only through sorrow.

Since the question inevitably concerns the prospects of the proposed marriage, the first statement of the problem is fully in harmony with the spirit of recent pragmatism. The truth of the assertion: "We ought to marry," is surely a truth that, as the pragmatists would say, the young lovers who make the assertion should regard as quite inseparable from the probable results to which this marriage will lead in concrete life. Such a truth then is, one would say, wholly empirical. A marriage proposal, to use the favourite phrase of pragmatism, is a "working hypothesis." Such hypotheses must be submitted to the test of experience. No such test, it would seem, would be absolute. What does poor humanity know as to the real values of our destiny? Meanwhile the whole problem of good and evil is in question. Marriage, especially under certain conditions, will lead to one or another sorrow. Can one face

sorrow with any really deeper trust in life? Is life
really a good at all, since there is so much sorrow
in it? Must not any prudent person be afraid of
life? Ought the lovers to defy fortune and to ignore
obvious worldly prudence?

Such is the first statement of the problem. Its
treatment in this admirable sketch shows an insight into the nature of good and evil which I had
myself come to regard as very little present to the
minds of the story-tellers of to-day, who are so often
dominated by the recent love of power, by the
tedious blindness of modern individualism, by false
doctrines as to the merely temporal expediency of
truth, and by the merely glittering show of unspiritual worldly efficiency. I rejoice to find that, in a
literature which has been, of late, so devastated by
a popularly trivial interpretation of pragmatism, and
by an equally trivial disregard for the "rule of reason," there is still place for so straightforward and
practical a recognition of eternal truth as the wise
woman who has written this short story exemplifies.

The issue regarding this particular marriage proposal is stated at once in the opening words of the
tale:

"Young Oliver Pickersgill was in love with Peter
Lannithorne's daughter. Peter Lannithorne was
serving a six-year term in the penitentiary for em-
bezzlement."

The young hero is depicted as a high-minded
youth of unquestionable and prosperous social posi-

tion in his community. His beloved is a loyal daughter who is convinced that her father's crime was due solely to a momentary and benevolent weakness, and to a mind confused by care for the needs and too importunate requirements of his own family. Not unjustly attributing the father's final downfall to the impatience, to the agonising discontent, and to the worldly ambition of her own mother, the daughter with spirit replies to the lover's proposal by saying plainly: "I will never marry any one who doesn't respect my father as I do." The lovers somewhat easily come to terms, at least apparently, as to this sole present ground for disagreement. The youth, not without inward difficulty, is ready to accept the daughter's version of her father's misadventure. In any case, love makes him indifferent to merely worldly scruples, and he has no fear of his own power to face his community as the loving husband of a convict's daughter; though there is, indeed, no doubt as to the father's actual guilt, and although Lannithorne is known to have admitted the justice of his sentence.

But to love, and to be magnanimously hopeful—this is not the same as to convince other people that such a marriage is prudent, or is likely, as the pragmatists would say, to have "expedient workings." Young Oliver has to persuade Ruth's mother on the one hand, his own father on the other, that such a marriage is reasonable. Both prove to be hard to convince. To the ordinary scruples of worldly pru-

dence which young lovers generally have to answer,
they easily add seemingly unanswerable objections.
The mother—the convict's wife—now a brilliantly
clear-witted but hopelessly narrow-minded invalid—
a broken woman of the world—pragmatically enlightened, in a way, by the bitter experience of
sorrow, but not in the least brought thereby to any
deeper insight, faces the lover as an intruder upon
her daughter's peace and her own desolation. She has
known, she says, what the bitterness of an unhappy
marriage can be and is. If she herself has had her
share of blame for her husband's downfall, that only
the more shows her such truth as, in this dark world,
she still can grasp. "I do not want my daughters to
marry"—this is, to her, the conclusion of the whole
matter. The bitterness of her own marriage has
taught her this lesson, which she expounds to the
lover with all the passion of wounded pride and the
dear-bought lore of life as she has learned it. But
of course, as she admits, she may be wrong. Let
the lover consult her husband at the jail. He—
the convict—is a well-meaning man, after all. He
fell; but he is not at heart a criminal. Let him
say whether he wants his daughter to take up the
burden of this new tragedy. So the mother concludes her parable.

The lover, baffled, but still hopeful, next turns to
his own father for consent and encouragement.
But now he has to listen to the teachings of a loftier
yet to him profoundly discouraging prudence. Oli-

ver's father is a truly high-minded man of the world, with a genuinely religious feeling in the background of his mind, and is intensely devoted to his son. But from this proposed match he recoils with a natural horror. The world is full of good girls. Why not choose one who brings no such sorrow with her? Peter Lannithorne was in his crime no worse, indeed, than many other men who are not in jail. He even meant on the whole well, and blundered, until at last from blunder he drifted into crime. He then took his penalty like a man, and owned that it was just. But, after all, he was found out. Such a taint lasts. It cannot be removed by repentance. The proposed marriage can only lead to misery. Peter Lannithorne himself, who, after all, "knows what's what," would be the first to admit this fact, if one asked his advice. If the son must persist in making light of a loving father's wisdom—well, let him then consult Peter Lannithorne himself. Ask the convict in his prison what a man needs and expects in the family of the woman whom he is to marry. This is the father's firm but kindly ultimatum.

Terrified by the gravity of repeated warnings, and dispirited by having to leave his dearest problem to the decision of the convict himself, Oliver determines to face the inevitable. He arranges for the interview at the jail, and is left by the warden alone with the prisoner in the prison library. Suddenly, as he faces his man, the youth finds himself in the presence of one who has somehow been transformed as if by a supernatural power.   As for the convict's person—

His features were irregular and unnoticeable; but the sum-total of them gave the impression of force.   It was a strong face, yet you could see that it had once been a weak one.   It was a tremendously human face, a face like a battle-ground, scarred and seamed and lined with the stress of invisible conflicts. . . . Not a triumphant face at all, and yet there was peace in it.   Somehow, the man had achieved something, arrived somewhere, and the record of the journey was piteous and terrible.   Yet it drew the eyes in awe as much as in wonder, and in pity not at all.

Oliver, reassured by the new presence, and glad to find himself at last facing a man who has nothing left to fear in life, states as well as possible his main problem.   The father of his beloved listens, first with surprise at the news, then with seriousness. Oliver finds himself forced to cut deep when he repeats his own father's appeal to know the convict's opinion about what a man expects to meet in his future wife's family, and then pauses with a keen sense of the cruelty of his own position.   But Lannithorne, who has long since become accustomed to feeling the ploughshare of passion grind down to his uttermost rock, is perfectly ready with his response.   As the youth pauses and then begins a new appeal—

The man looked up and held up an arresting hand.   "Let me clear the way for you a little," he said.   "It was a hard thing for you to come and seek me out in this place. I like your coming. Most young men would have refused, or come in a different spirit. I want you to understand that if in Ruth's eyes, and my wife's, and your father's, my counsel has value, it is because they think I see things as they are. And that means, first of all, that I know myself for a man who committed a crime and is paying the penalty. I am satisfied to be paying it. As I see justice, it is just. So, if I seem to wince at your necessary allusions to it, that is part of the price. I don't want you to feel that you are blundering or hurting me more than is necessary. You have got to lay the thing before me as it is."

Something in the words, in the dry, patient manner, in the endurance of the man's face, touched Oliver to the quick and made him feel all manner of new things: such as a sense of the moral poise of the universe, acquiescence in its retributions, and a curious pride, akin to Ruth's own, in a man who could meet him after this fashion, in this place.

Hereupon, fully aroused, the youth tells with freedom why the problem seems so hard for the young people, and how their elders all insist upon such frightful discouragements, and how much he longs to know the truth about life, and whether all such doubts and scruples as those of his own father and of Ruth's mother are well founded. At last the prisoner begins his reply:

"They haven't the point of view," he said. "It is life that is the great adventure. Not love, not marriage, not business. They are just chapters in the book. The main thing is to take the road fearlessly—to have courage to live one's life."

"Courage?"

Lannithorne nodded.

"That is the great word. Don't you see what ails your father's point of view, and my wife's? One wants absolute security in one way for Ruth; the other wants absolute security in another way for you. And security—why, it's just the one thing a human being can't have, the thing that's the damnation of him if he gets it! The reason it is so hard for a rich man to enter the Kingdom of Heaven is that he has that false sense of security. To demand it just disintegrates a man. I don't know why. It does."

Oliver shook his head uncertainly.

"I don't quite follow you, sir. Oughtn't one to try to be safe?"

"One ought to try, yes. That is common prudence. But the point is that, whatever you do or get, you aren't after all secure. There is no such condition, and the harder you demand it, the more risk you run. So it is up to a man to take all reasonable precautions about his money, or his happiness, or his life, and trust the rest. What every man in the world is looking for is the sense of having the mastery over life. But I tell you, boy, there is only one thing that really gives it!"

"And that is——?"

Lannithorne hesitated perceptibly. For the thing he was about to tell this undisciplined lad was his most precious possession; it was the price of wisdom for which he had paid with the years of his life. No man parts lightly with such knowledge.

"It comes," he said, with an effort, "with the knowledge of our power to endure. That's it. *You are safe only when you can stand everything that can happen to you.* Then, and then only! Endurance is the measure of a man! . . . Sometimes I think it is harder to endure what we deserve, like me," said Lannithorne, "than what we don't. I was afraid, you see, afraid for my wife and all of them. Anyhow, take my word for it. Courage is security. There is no other kind."

"Then—Ruth and I——"

"Ruth is the core of my heart!" said Lannithorne thickly. "I would rather die than have her suffer more than she must. But she must take her chances like the rest. It is the law of things. If you know yourself fit for her, and feel reasonably sure you can take care of her, you have a right to trust the future. Myself, I believe there is some One to trust it to."

The speaker of this hard-won wisdom, after this appeal to the eternal, utters his last tremulous word as from a father's loving heart, and then the interview must end. The author concludes:

Finding his way out of the prison yard a few minutes later, Oliver looked, unseeing, at the high walls that soared against the blue spring sky. He could not realise them, there was such a sense of light, air, space, in his spirit.

Apparently, he was just where he had been an hour before, with all his battles still to fight, but really he knew they were already won, for his weapon had been forged and put in his hand. He left his boyhood behind him as he passed that stern threshold, for the last hour had made a man of him, and a prisoner had given him the master-key that opens every door.

VI

Now this, I insist, is insight. It is no "soft" doctrine. It is far beyond the sort of pragmatism that accepts the test of momentary results. As far as it goes, it is religious insight. It is insight, moreover, into the nature of certain ills which cannot, yes, which in principle, and even by omnipotence, could not, be simply removed from existence without abolishing the conditions which are logically necessary to the very highest good that we know. Life in the spirit simply presupposes the conditions that these ills exemplify.

What sorrow is deeper than the full recognition of one's own now irrevocable deed, if one has, hereupon, fully to confess that this deed is, from one's own present point of view, a crime? Yet how could such ills be simply removed from existence if any range of individual expression, of freedom, of power to choose is to be left open at all? How can one possess spiritual effectiveness—the privilege that youth most ardently demands—without assuming the risk involved in taking personal responsibility for some aspects of the lives of our fellows? As for our blunders, what more precious privilege do we all claim than the privilege of making our own blunders, or at least a due proportion of them? When we act, every act is done for eternity, since it is irrevocable. When we love, we ask the privilege to bind up other destinies with our own. The tragedies of such a world as ours are, therefore, not such as could be simply wiped out of existence, unless one were ready to deprive every individual personality both of its range of free choice and of its effectiveness of action. When we suffer, then, in such a world, we know indeed that there need have been no such suffering had there been no world at all. But precisely when our ills are most bound up with

our own personal wills, we know that no mere re-
moval of such ills could have occurred without the
abolition of all the conditions which our spiritual
freedom, our longing for effectiveness, and our love
for union with other personalities make us regard
as the conditions of the highest good.   No God could
conceivably give you the good of self-expression
without granting you the privilege, not only of
choosing wrongly, but of involving your brethren in
the results of your misdeed.   For when you love
your kind, you aim to be a factor in their lives; and
to deprive you of this privilege would be to insure
your total failure.   But if you possess this privilege,
you share in a life that, in proportion to its importance and depth and range and richness of spiritual
relations, is full of the possibilities of tragedy.

Face such tragedy, however, and what does it
show you?   The possibility, not of annulling an
evil, or of ceasing to regret it, but of showing spiritual power, first, through idealising your grief, by
seeing even through this grief the depth of the significance of our relations as individuals to one another, to our social order, and to the whole of life;
secondly, through enduring your fortune; and thirdly,
through conquering, by the might of the spirit, those
goods which can only be won through such sorrow.
What those goods are, the convict has just, if only
in small part, told us.   Griselda told us something
about them which is much deeper still.   For adversity and loyalty are, indeed, simply inseparable

companions. There could not be loyalty in a world
where the loyal being himself met no adversities
that personally belonged to and entered his own
inner life. That this is true, let every loyal experience bear witness.

Now such sorrows, such idealised evils, which are
so interwoven with good that if the precious grief
were wholly removed from existence, the courage,
the fidelity, the spiritual self-possession, the peace
through and in and beyond tribulation which such
trials alone make possible, would also be removed—
they surely show us that the abstract principle:
"Evil ought to be abolished," is false. They show
us that the divine will also must be made perfect
through suffering. Since we can comprehend the
meaning of such experiences only through resolute
action, through courage, through loyalty, through
the power of the spirit, they in no wise justify sloth,
or mere passivity, or mystical idleness. The active
dealing with such sorrow gives, as James himself
once well asserts, a new dimension to life. No experiences go further than do these to show us how,
in our loyalty and in our courage, we are becoming
one with the master of life, who through sorrow
overcomes.

Let man, the destroyer, then remember that there
is one ill which he could not destroy, even if he were
God, without also destroying all the spiritual
prowess in which all those rejoice who, inspired by
an ambition infinitely above that of Achilles, long

to be one with God through bearing and overcoming the sorrows of a world.

We have thus indicated a source of insight. To tell more about what it reveals would at once lead me, as you see, close to the most vital of all Christian teachings, the doctrine of the Atonement. But such a study belongs elsewhere.

VII

THE UNITY OF THE SPIRIT AND THE
INVISIBLE CHURCH

VII

THE UNITY OF THE SPIRIT AND THE INVISIBLE CHURCH

My present and concluding lecture must begin with some explanations of what I mean by the term "The Unity of the Spirit." Then I shall have to define my use of the term "The Invisible Church." Thereafter, we shall be free to devote ourselves to the consideration of a source of religious insight as omnipresent as it is variously interpreted by those who, throughout all the religious world, daily appeal to its guidance. The outcome of our discussion may help some of you, as I hope, to turn your attention more toward the region where the greatest help is to be found in the cultivation of that true loyalty which, if I am right, is the heart and core of every higher religion.

I

In these lectures I have repeatedly called the religious objects, that is, the objects whereof the knowledge tends to the salvation of man, "superhuman" and "supernatural" objects. I have more or less fully explained, as I went, the sense in which

I hold these objects to be both superhuman and supernatural. But every use of familiar traditional terms is likely to arouse misunderstandings. I have perfectly definite reasons for my choice of the traditional words in question as adjectives wherewith to characterise the religious objects. But I do not want to leave in your minds any doubts as to what my usage is deliberately intended to imply. I do not want to seem to make any wrong use of the vaguer associations which will be in your minds when something human is compared with something superhuman, and when the natural and the supernatural are contrasted. This closing lecture, in which I am to deal with an aspect of spiritual life which we have everywhere in our discourse tacitly presupposed, but which now is to take its definitive place on our list of sources of religious insight, gives me my best opportunity to forestall useless misunderstandings by putting myself upon record as to the precise sense in which both the new source itself and everything else superhuman and supernatural to which religion has a rational right to appeal is, to my mind, a reality, and is a source or an object of human insight. I shall therefore explain the two adjectives just emphasised by giving you a somewhat fuller account of their sense than I have heretofore stated. If the new account touches upon technical matters, I hope that, by our long list of illustrations of the superhuman and of the supernatural, we have now sufficiently prepared the way.

In my general sketch of the characteristics of human nature which awaken in us the sense of our need for salvation, I laid stress, both in our first and in our second lectures, upon our narrowness of outlook as one principal and pervasive defect of man as he naturally is constituted. I illustrated this narrowness by some of its most practically noteworthy instances. Repeatedly I returned, in later discussions, to this same feature of our life. Now man's narrowness of natural outlook upon life is first of all due to something which I have to call the "form" of human consciousness. What I mean by this form, I have already illustrated to you freely by the very instances to which I have just referred. But technical clearness as to such topics is hard to attain. Allow me, then, to insist with some care upon matters which are as influential in moulding our whole destiny as they are commonly neglected in our discussions of the problems of life and of reality.

Man can attend to but a very narrow range of facts at any one instant. Common-sense observation shows you this. Psychological experiment emphasises it in manifold ways. Listen to a rhythmic series of beats—drum beats—or the strokes of an engine, or the feet of horses passing by in the street. You cannot directly grasp with entire clearness more than a very brief sequence of these beats, or other sounds, or of rhythmic phrases of any kind. If the rhythm of a regularly repeated set of sounds is too long, or too complex, it becomes confused for you. You cannot make out by your direct attention what it is at least until it has by repetition grown familiar. Let several objects be brought before you at once. You can attend to one and then to another at pleasure if only they stay there to be attended to. But only a very few distinct objects can be suddenly seen at once, and at a single glance, and recognised, through that one instantaneous presentation, for what they are. If the objects are revealed to you in the darkness by an electric spark, or are seen through a single slit in a screen that rapidly moves before your eyes—so that the objects are exposed to your observation only during the extremely brief time when the slit passes directly between them and your eyes—this limit of your power to grasp several distinct objects at once, upon a single inspection, can be experimentally tested. The results of such experiments concern us here only in the most general way. Enough—as such tests show—what one may call the *span* of our consciousness, its power to grasp many facts in any one individual moment of our lives, is extremely limited. It is limited as to the number of simultaneously presented facts that we can grasp at one view, can distinguish, and recognise, and hold clearly before us. It is also limited with regard to the number and the duration of the successive facts that we can so face as directly to grasp the character of their succession, rhythmic or otherwise.

Now this limitation of the span of our consciousness is, I repeat, an ever-present defect of our human type of conscious life. That is why I call it a defect in the "form" of our conscious life. It is not a defect limited to the use of any one of our senses. It is not a failure of eyes or of ears to furnish to us a sufficient variety of facts to observe. On the contrary, both our eyes and our ears almost constantly rain in upon us, especially during our more desultory waking life, an overwealth of impressions. If we want to know facts, and to attain clearness, we have to pick out a few of these impressions, from instant to instant, for more careful direct inspection. In any case, then, this limitation is not due to the defects of our senses. It is our whole conscious make-up, our characteristic way of becoming aware of things, which is expressed by this limitation of our conscious span. On this plan our human consciousness is formed. Thus our type of awareness is constituted. In this way we are all doomed to live. It is our human fate to grasp clearly only a few facts or ideas at any one instant. And so, being what we are, we have to make the best of our human nature.

Meanwhile, it is of our very essence as reasonable beings that we are always contending with the consequences of this our natural narrowness of span. We are always actively rebelling at our own form of consciousness, so long as we are trying to know or to do anything significant. We want to grasp many things at once, not merely a few. We want to survey life in long stretches, not merely in instantaneous glimpses. We are always like beings who have to see our universe through the cracks that our successive instants open before us, and as quickly close again. And we want to see things, *not* through these instantaneous cracks, but without intervening walls, with wide outlook, and in all their true variety and unity. Nor is this rebellion of ours against the mere form of consciousness any merely idle curiosity or peevish seeking for a barren wealth of varieties. Salvation itself is at stake in this struggle for a wider clearness of outlook. The wisest souls, as we have throughout seen, agree with common-sense prudence in the desire to see at any one instant greater varieties of ideas and of objects than our form of consciousness permits us to grasp. To escape from the limitations imposed upon us by the natural narrowness of our span of consciousness— by the form of consciousness in which we live—this is the common interest of science and of religion, of the more contemplative and of the more active aspects of our higher nature. *Our form of consciousness is one of our chief human sorrows.*

By devices such as the rhythmic presentation of facts to our attention we can do something—not very much—to enlarge our span of consciousness. But for most purposes we can make only an *indirect,* not a *direct,* escape from our limitations of span. Our salvation depends upon the winning of such

indirect successes. Indirectly we escape, in so far
as we use our powers of habit-forming, of memory,
and of abstraction, to prepare for us objects of momentary experience such as have come to acquire for
us a wide range of meaning, so that, when we get
before our momentary attention but a few of these
objects at once, we still are able to comprehend,
after our human fashion, ranges and connections
and unities of fact which the narrow form of our
span of consciousness forbids us to grasp with
directness. Thus, the repetition of similar experiences forms habits such that each element of some
new instant of passing experience comes to us sat-
urated with the meaning that, as we look back upon
our past life, we suppose to have resulted from the
whole course of what has happened. And through
such endlessly varied processes of habit-forming,
we come to reach stages of insight in which the instantaneous presentation of a few facts gets for us,
at a given moment, the value of an indirect appreciation of what we never directly grasp—that is, the
value of a wide survey of life. All that we usually
call knowledge is due to such indirect grasping of
what the instant can only hint to us, although we
usually feel as if this indirect presentation were itself a direct insight. Let me exemplify: The odour
of a flower may come to us burdened with a meaning that we regard as the total result of a whole
summer of our life. The wrinkled face of an old
man reveals to us, in its momentarily presented

traces, the signs of what we take to have been his lifetime's experience and slowly won personal character. And, in very much the same way, almost any passing experience may seem to us to speak with the voice of years, or even of ages, of human life. To take yet another instance: a single musical chord epitomises the result of all our former hearings of the musical composition which it introduces.

In this way we live, despite our narrowness, *as if* we saw widely; and we constantly view *as if it were* our actual experience, a sense and connection of things which actually never gets fully translated in any moment of our lives, but is always simply presupposed as the interpretation which a wider view of life *would* verify. Thus bounded in the nutshell of the passing instant, we count ourselves (in one way or another, and whatever our opinions), kings of the infinite realm of experience, or would do so were it not that, like Hamlet, we have so many "bad dreams," which make us doubt the correctness of our interpretations, and feel our need of an escape from this stubborn natural prison of our own form of consciousness. We therefore appeal, in all our truth-seeking, to a wider view than our own present view.

Our most systematic mode of indirect escape from the consequences of our narrow span of consciousness, is the mode which our thinking processes, that is, our dealings with abstract and general ideas exemplify.

Such abstract and general ideas, as we earlier saw, are means to ends—never ends in themselves. By means of generalisation or abstraction we can gradually come to choose signs which we can more or less successfully substitute for long series of presented objects of experience; and we can also train ourselves into active ways of estimating or of describing things —ways such, that by reminding ourselves of these our active attitudes toward the business of life, we can seem to ourselves to epitomise in an instant the sense of years or even of ages of human experience. Such signs and symbols and attitudes constitute our store of general and abstract ideas. Our more or less systematic and voluntary thinking is a process of observing, at one or another instant, the connections and the meanings of a very few of these our signs and attitudes at once. We actively put together these ideas of ours, and watch, at the instant, the little connections that then and there are able to appear, despite the narrowness of our span of consciousness. That, for instance, is what happens when we add up columns of figures, or think out a problem, or plan our practical lives. But because each of the ideas used, each of these signs or symbols or attitudes, can be more or less safely substituted for some vast body of facts of experience, what we observe only in and through our narrow span can indirectly help us to appreciate something whose real meaning only a very wide range of experience, a consciousness whose span is enormously vaster than ours, could possibly present directly.

Thus, confined to our own form and span of consciousness as we are, we spend our lives in acquiring or devising ways to accomplish indirectly what we are forbidden directly to attain, namely, the discovery of truth and of meaning such as only a consciousness of another form than ours can realise. Now, as I maintained in our third and fourth lectures, *the whole validity and value of this indirect procedure of ours depends upon the principle that such a wider view of things, such a larger unity of consciousness, such a direct grasp of the meanings at which we indirectly but ceaselessly aim is a reality in the universe.* As I there maintained, *the whole reality of the universe itself must be defined, in terms of the reality of such an inclusive and direct grasp of the whole sense of things.* I can here only repeat my opinion that this thesis is one which nobody can deny without self-contradiction.

Now the difference between the narrow form of consciousness that we human beings possess and the wider and widest forms of consciousness whose reality every common-sense effort to give sense to life, and every scientific effort to discover the total verdict of experience presupposes—the difference, I say, between these two forms of consciousness is *literally* expressed by calling the one form (the form that we all possess) *human*, and by calling the other form (the form of a wider consciousness which views experience as it is) *superhuman.* The wider conscious view of things that we share only indirectly, through the devices just pointed out, is certainly not human; for no mortal man ever directly possesses it. It is real; for, as we saw in our study of the reason, if you deny this assertion in one shape, you reaffirm it in another. For you can define the truth and falsity of your own opinions only by presupposing a wider view that sees as a whole what you see in fragments. That unity of consciousness which we presuppose in all our indirect efforts to get into touch with its direct view of truth is above our level. It includes what we actually get before us in our form of consciousness. It also includes all that we are trying to grasp indirectly. Now what is not human, and is above our level, and includes all of our insight, but transcends and corrects our indirect efforts by its direct grasp of facts as they are, can best be called superhuman. *The thesis that such a superhuman consciousness is a reality is a thesis precisely equivalent to the assertion that our experience has any real sense or connection whatever* beyond the mere fragment of connectedness that, at any one instant, we directly grasp.

Furthermore, to call such a larger consciousness— inclusive of our own, but differing from ours, in form, by the vastness of its span and the variety and completeness of the connections that it surveys —to call it, I say, a *supernatural* consciousness is to use a phraseology that can be very deliber-

ately and, if you choose, technically defended. By
"natural" we mean simply: Subject to the laws
which hold for the sorts of beings whose character
and behaviour our empirical sciences can study. If
you suddenly found that you could personally and
individually and clearly grasp, by an act of direct
attention, the sense and connection of thousands of
experiences at once, instead of the three or four
presented facts of experience whose relations you
can now directly observe in any one of your moments of consciousness, you would indeed say that
you had been miraculously transformed into another type of being whose insight had acquired an
angelic sort of wealth and clearness. But whenever you assert (as every scientific theory, and every
common-sense opinion, regarding the real connections of the facts of human experience requires you
to assert), that not only thousands, but a countless collection of data of human experience actually
possess a perfectly coherent total sense and meaning, such as no individual man ever directly observes,
this your assertion, which undertakes to be a report
of facts, and which explicitly relates to facts of experience, implies the assertion that there exists such
a superhuman survey of the real nature and connection of our own natural realm of conscious life.
We ourselves are strictly limited by the natural
conditions that determine our own form of consciousness. And no conditions can be regarded by us as
more characteristically natural than are these. For

us human beings to transcend those conditions, by surveying countless data at once, would require an uttermost exception to the natural laws which are found to govern our human type of consciousness. To believe that any man ever had accomplished the direct survey of the whole range of the physical connections of the solar and stellar systems at once— in other words, had grasped the whole range of astronomical experience in a single act of attention— would be to believe that a most incredible miracle had at some time taken place—an incredible miracle so far as any knowledge that we now possess enables us to foresee what the natural conditions under which man lives, and is, in human form, conscious, permit. But, on the other hand, to accept, as we all do, the validity of that scientific interpretation of the data of human experience which astronomy reports is to acknowledge that such an interpretation more or less completely records a system of facts which are nothing if they are not in some definite sense empirical, although, in their wholeness, they are experienced by no man. That is, the acceptance of the substantial truth of astronomy involves the acknowledgment that some such, to us simply superhuman, consciousness is precisely as real as the stars are real, and as their courses, and as all their relations are real. Yet, of course, we cannot undertake to investigate any process such as would enable us to define the natural conditions under which any such superhuman survey of astronomical facts would become psychologically possible.

The acceptance of our natural sciences, as valid interpretations of connections of experience which our form of consciousness forbids us directly to verify, logically presupposes, at every step, that such superhuman forms and unities of consciousness are real. For the facts of science are indefinable except as facts in and for a real experience. But, on the other hand, we can hope for no advance in physical or in psychological knowledge which would enable us to bring these higher forms of consciousness under what we call natural laws. So the superhuman forms of consciousness remain for us also supernatural. *That* they are, we must acknowledge, if any assertion whatever about our world is to be either true or false. For all assertions are made about experience, and about its real connections, and about its systems. But *what* conditions, *what* natural causes, bring such superhuman forms of consciousness into existence we are unable to investigate. For every assertion about nature or about natural laws presupposes that natural facts and laws are real only in so far as they are the objects known to such higher unities of consciousness. The unities in question are themselves no natural objects; while all natural facts are objects for them and are expressions of their meaning.

Thus definite are my reasons for asserting that forms of consciousness superior to our own are real, and that they are all finally united in a single, world-embracing insight, which has also the character of expressing a world-will. Thus definite are also my grounds for calling such higher unities of consciousness both superhuman and supernatural. By the term "The unity of the spirit" I name simply *the unity of meaning which belongs to these superhuman forms of consciousness.* We ourselves partake of this unity, and share it, in so far as, in our lives also, we discover and express, in whatever way our own form of consciousness permits, truth and life that bring us into touch and into harmony with the higher forms of consciousness, that is, with the spirit which, in its wholeness, knows and estimates the world, and which expresses itself in the life of the world.

Thus near are we, in every exercise of our reasonable life, to the superhuman and to the supernatural. Upon the other hand, there is positively no need of magic, or of miracle, or of mysterious promptings from the subconscious, to prove to us the reality of the human and of the supernatural, or to define our reasonable relations with it. And the essential difference between our own type of consciousness and this higher life is a difference of form, and is also a difference of content precisely in so far as its wider and widest span of conscious insight implies that the superhuman type of consciousness possesses a depth of meaning, a completeness of expression, a wealth of facts, a clearness of vision, a successful embodiment of purpose which, in view of the narrowness of our form of consciousness, do not belong to us.

Man needs no miracles to show him the supernatural and the superhuman. You need no signs and wonders, and no psychical research, to prove that the unity of the spirit is a fact in the world. Common-sense tacitly presupposes the reality of the unity of the spirit. Science studies the ways in which its life is expressed in the laws which govern the order of experience. Reason gives us insight into its real being. Loyalty serves it, and repents not of the service. Salvation means our positive harmony with its purpose and with its manifestation.

II

Amongst the sources of insight which bring us into definite and practical relations with that spiritual world whose nature has now been again defined, one of the most effective is the life and the word of other men who are minded to be loyal to genuine causes, and who are already, through the service of their common causes, brought together in some form of spiritual brotherhood. The real unity of the life of such fellow-servants of the Spirit is itself an instance of a superhuman conscious reality; and its members are devoted to bringing themselves into harmony with the purposes of the universe. Any brotherhood of men who thus loyally live in the Spirit is, from my point of view, a brotherhood essentially religious in its nature, precisely in proportion as it is practically moved by an effort to serve—not merely the special cause to which its members, because of their training and their traditions, happen to be devoted, but also the common cause of all the loyal. Such a brotherhood, so far as it is indeed human, and, therefore narrow, may not very expressly define what this common cause of all the loyal is, for its members may not be thoughtfully reflective people. But if, while rejoicing in their own perfectly real fraternal unity, they are also practically guided by the love of furthering brotherhood amongst men in general; if they respect the loyalty of other men so far as they understand that loyalty; if they seek, not to sow discord amongst the brethren of our communities, but to be a city set on a hill, that not only cannot be hid, but is also a model for other cities—a centre for the spreading of the spirit of loyalty—then the members of such an essentially fruitful brotherhood are actually loyal to the cause of causes. They are a source of insight to all who know of their life, and who rightly appreciate its meaning. And of such is the kingdom of loyalty. And the communities which such men form and serve are essentially religious communities. Each one is an example of the unity of the Spirit. Each one stands for a reality that belongs to the superhuman world.

Since the variety of social forms which appear under human conditions is an unpredictably vast variety, and since the motives which guide men are endlessly complex, different communities of loyal people may possess such a religious character and value in the most various degrees. For it results from the narrowness of the human form of consciousness that men, at any one moment, know not the whole of what they mean. No sharp line can be drawn sundering the brotherhoods and partnerships, and other social organisations which men devise, into those which for the men concerned are consciously religious, and those which, by virtue of their absence of interest in the larger and deeper loyalties are secular. The test whereby such a distinction should be made is in principle a definite test. But to apply the test to every possible case requires a searching of human hearts and a just estimate of deeds and motives whereto, in our ignorance, we are very generally inadequate.

A business firm would seem to be, in general, no model of a religious organisation. Yet it justly demands loyalty from its members and its servants. If it lives and acts merely for gain, it is secular indeed. But if its business is socially beneficent, if its cause is honourable, if its dealings are honest, if its treatment of its allies and rivals is such as makes for the confidence, the cordiality, and the stability of the whole commercial life of its community and (when its influence extends so far) of the world, if

public spirit and true patriotism inspire its doings,
if it is always ready on occasion to sacrifice gain for
honour's sake—then there is no reason why it may
not become and be a genuinely and fervently religious brotherhood. Certainly a family can become
a religious organisation; and some of the most ancient traditions of mankind have demanded that it
should be one. There is also, and justly, a religion
of patriotism, which regards the country as a divine institution. Such a religion serves the unity
of the spirit in a perfectly genuine way. Some of
the most momentous religious movements in the
world's history have grown out of such an idealised
patriotism. Christianity, in transferring local names
from Judea to a heavenly world, has borne witness
to the sacredness that patriotism, upon its higher
levels, acquires.

In brief, the question whether a given human
brotherhood is a religious institution or not is a
question for that brotherhood to decide for itself,
subject only to the truth about its real motives.
Has its cause the characters that mark a fitting
cause of loyalty? Does it so serve its cause as
thereby to further the expression of the divine unity
of the spirit in the form of devoted human lives, not
only within its own brotherhood, but as widely as
its influence extends? Then it is an essentially religious organisation. Nor does the extent of its
worldly influence enable you to decide how far it
meets these requirements. Nor yet does the num-

ber of persons in its membership form any essential criterion. Wherever two or three are gathered together, and are living as they can in the Spirit that the divine will (which wills the loyal union of all mankind) requires of them—there, indeed, the work of the Spirit is done; and the organisation in question is a religious brotherhood. It needs no human sanction to make it such. Though it dwell on a desert island, and though all its members soon die and are forgotten of men, its loyal deeds are irrevocable facts of the eternal world; and the universal life knows that here at least the divine will is expressed in human acts.

But so far as such communities both exist and are distinctly recognisable as religious in their life and intent, they form a source of religious insight to all who come under their influence. Such a source acts as a means whereby any or all of our previous sources may be opened to us, may become effective, may bear fruit. *Hence, in this new source, we find the crowning source of religious insight.*

This last statement is one which is accepted by many who would nevertheless limit its application to certain religious communities, and to those only; or who, in some cases, would limit its application to some one religious community. There are, for instance, many who say, for various special reasons, that the crowning source of religious insight is the visible church. By this term those who use it in any of its traditional senses, mean one religious institution only, or at most only a certain group of religious organisations. The visible church is a religious organisation, or group of such organisations, which is characterised by certain traditions, by a certain real or supposed history, by a more or less well-defined creed, and by further assertions concerning the divine revelation to which it owes its origin and authority. With the doctrinal questions involved in the understanding of this definition, these lectures, as you now well know, have no direct concern. It is enough for our present purpose to say that the visible church thus defined is indeed, and explicitly, and in our present sense, a religious organisation. In all those historical forms which here concern us, the visible church has undertaken to show men the way to salvation. It has carried out its task by uniting its members in a spiritual brotherhood. It has in ideal extended its interest to all mankind. It has aimed at universal brotherhood. It has defined and called out loyalty. It has conceived this loyalty as a service of God and as a loyalty to the cause of all mankind. Its traditions, the lives of its servants, its services, its teachings, have been and are an inexhaustible source of religious insight to the vast multitudes whom it has influenced and, in its various forms and embodiments, still influences. Not unnaturally, therefore, those who accept its own doctrines regarding its origin and history view such a visible church not only as by far the most important source of religious in-

sight, but also as a source occupying an entirely
unique position.

The deliberate limitations of the undertaking of
these lectures forbid me, as I have just reminded
you, to consider in any detail this supposed unique-
ness of the position which so many of you will as-
sign to some form of the historical Christian church.
After what I have said as to the nature and the
variety of the forms which the spiritual life has
taken, and still takes, amongst men, you will nevertheless not be surprised if, without attempting to
judge the correctness of the traditions of the visible
church, I forthwith point out that, to the higher religious life of mankind the life of the visible church
stands related as part to whole; and that very vast
ranges of the higher religious life of mankind have
grown and flourished outside of the influence of
Christianity. And when the religious life of mankind is viewed in its historical connections, truth
requires us to insist that Christianity itself has been
dependent for its insight and its power upon many
different sources, some of which assumed human
form not only long before Christianity came into
being, but in nations and in civilisations which were
not dependent for their own spiritual wealth upon
the Jewish religious traditions that Christianity
itself undertook to transform and to assimilate.
Christianity is, in its origins, not only Jewish but
Hellenic, both as to its doctrines and as to its type
of spirituality. It is a synthesis of religious motives

which had their sources widely spread throughout the pre-Christian world of Hellenism. Its own insight is partly due to the non-Christian world.

As a fact, then, the unity of the Spirit, the religious life which has been and is embodied in the form of human fraternities, is the peculiar possession of no one time, or nation, and belongs to no unique and visible church. Yet such an unity is a source of religious insight. We have a right to use it wherever we find it and however it becomes accessible to us. As a fact, we all use such insight without following any one principle as to the selection of the historical sources. Socrates and Plato and Sophocles are religious teachers from whom we have all directly or indirectly learned, whether we know it or not. Our own Germanic ancestors, and the traditions of the Roman Empire, have influenced our type of loyalty and have taught us spiritual truth that we should not otherwise know.

Moreover, that which I have called the cause of all the loyal, the real unity of the whole spiritual world, is not merely a moral ideal. It is a religious reality. Its servants and ministers are present wherever religious brotherhood finds sincere and hearty manifestation. In the sight of a perfectly real but superhuman knowledge of the real purposes and effective deeds of mankind, *all the loyal, whether they individually know the fact or not, are, and in all times have been, one genuine and religious brotherhood.* Human narrowness and the vicissi-

tudes of the world of time have hidden, and still
hide, the knowledge of this community of the loyal
from human eyes.   But indirectly it comes to light
whenever the loyalty of one visible spiritual community comes, through any sort of tradition, or cus-
tom, or song or story, or wise word or noble deed, to
awaken new manifestations of the loyal life in faithful souls anywhere amongst men.

*I call the community of all who have sought for sal-
vation through loyalty the Invisible Church.*   What
makes it invisible to us is our ignorance of the facts
of human history and, still more, our narrowness in
our appreciation of spiritual truth.   And I merely
report the genuine facts, human and superhuman,
when I say that *whatever any form of the visible church
has done or will do for the religious life of mankind,
the crowning source of religious insight is, for us all,
the actual loyalty, service, devotion, suffering, accom-
plishment, traditions, example, teaching, and triumphs
of the invisible church of all the faithful.*   And by the
invisible church I mean the brotherhood consisting
of all who, in any clime or land, live in the Spirit.

Our terms have now been, so far as my time permits, sharply defined.   I am here not appealing to
vague sentiments about human brotherhood, or to
merely moral ideals about what we merely hope that
man may yet come to be.   And I am not for a moment committing myself to any mere worship of
humanity, so long as one conceives humanity as the
mere collection of those who are subject to the nat-

ural laws that govern our present physical and mental existence. Humanity, viewed as a mere product of nature, is narrow-minded and degraded enough. Its life is full of uncomprehended evils and of mutual misunderstandings. It is not a fitting object of any religious reverence. But it needs salvation. It has been finding salvation through loyalty. And the true cause, the genuine community, the real spiritual brotherhood of the loyal is a superhuman and not merely a human reality. It expresses itself in the lives of the loyal. In so far as these expressions directly or indirectly inspire our own genuine loyalty, they give us insight. Of such insight, whatever you may learn from communion with any form of the visible church, is an instance—a special embodiment. The invisible church, then, is no merely human and secular institution. It is a real and superhuman organisation. It includes and transcends every form of the visible church. It is the actual subject to which belong all the spiritual gifts which we can hope to enjoy. If your spiritual eyes were open, no diversity of human tongues, no strangeness of rites or of customs or of other forms of service, no accidental quaintnesses of tradition or of symbols or of creeds, would hide from your vision its perfections. It believes everywhere in the unity of the Spirit, and aims to save men through winning them over to the conscious service of its own unity. And it grants you the free grace of whatever religious insight you can acquire from outside yourself.

If you are truly religious, you live in it and for it. You conceive its life in your own way and, no doubt, under the limitations of your own time and creed. But you cannot flee from its presence. And your salvation lies in its reality, in your service, and in your communion with its endlessly varied company of those who suffer and who in the might of the spirit overcome.

Let me tell you something of this life of the invisible church.

III

And first let me speak of its membership. We have now repeatedly defined the test of such membership. The invisible church is the spiritual brotherhood of the loyal. Only a searcher of hearts can quite certainly know who are the really loyal. We can be sure regarding the nature of loyalty. That loyalty itself should come to men's consciousness in the most various forms and degrees, and clouded by the most tragic misunderstandings, the narrow form of human consciousness, and the blindness and variety of human passion, make necessary.

If one is loyal to a narrow and evil cause, as the robber or the pirate may be loyal to his band or to his ship, a conscious effort to serve the unity of the whole spiritual world may seem at first sight to be excluded by the nature of the loyalty in question. But what makes a cause evil, and unworthy of loyal

service, is the fact that its service is destructive of
the causes of other men, so that the evil cause preys
upon the loyalty of the spiritual brethren of those
who serve it, and so that thereby the servants of
this cause do actual wrong to mankind. But this
very fact may not be understood by the individual
robber or pirate. He may be devoted with all his
heart and soul and mind and strength to the best
cause that he knows. He may therefore sincerely
conceive that the master of life authorises his cause.
In that case, and so far as this belief is sincere, the
robber or pirate may be a genuinely religious man.

Does this statement seem to you an absurd quib-
ble? Then look over the past history of mankind.
Some at least of the Crusaders were genuinely religious. That we all readily admit. But they were
obviously, for the most part, robbers and murderers,
and sometimes pirates, of what we should now think
the least religious type if they were to-day sailing
the Mediterranean or devastating the lands. Read
in "Hakluyt's Voyages" the accounts of the spirit
in which the English explorers and warriors of the
Elizabethan age accomplished their great work.   In
these accounts a genuinely religious type of patriotism and of Christianity often expresses itself side
by side with a reckless hatred of the Spaniard and
a ferocity which tolerates the most obvious expressions of mere natural greed. These heroes of the
beginnings of the British Empire often hardly knew
whether they were rather the adventurous mer-

chants, or the loyal warriors for England, or the defenders of the Christian faith, or simply pirates. In fact they were all these things at once. Consider the Scottish clans as they were up to the eighteenth century. The spirit that they fostered has since found magnificent expression in the loyalty of the Scottish people and in its later and far-reaching service of some of the noblest causes that men know. Yet these clans loved cattle-thieving and tortured their enemies. When did they *begin* to be really patriots and servants of mankind? When did they begin to be truly and heartily religious? Who of us can tell?

Greed and blindness are natural to man. His form of consciousness renders him unable, in many cases, to realise their unreasonableness, even when he has already come into sincerely spiritual relations with the cause of all the loyal. What we *can* know is that greed and blindness are never of themselves religious, and that the way of salvation is the way of loyalty. But I know not what degrees of greedy blindness are consistent with an actual membership in the invisible church, as I have just defined its membership. When I meet, however, with the manifestations of the spirit of universal loyalty, whether in clansman, or in crusader, or in Elizabethan and piratical English defender of his country's faith, or in the Spaniard whom he hated, I hope that I may be able to use, not the greed or the passions of these people, but their re-

ligious prowess, their free surrender of themselves
to their cause, as a source of insight.

Membership in the invisible church is therefore
not to be determined by mere conventions, but by
the inward spirit of the faithful, as expressed in
their loyal life according to their lights. Yet of
those who seem to us most clearly to belong to the
service of the spirit, it is easy to enumerate certain
very potent groups, to whose devotion we all owe
an unspeakably great debt. The sages, the poets,
the prophets, whose insight we consulted in our
opening lecture, and have used throughout these
discourses, form such groups. It is indifferent to
us to what clime or land or tongue or visible religious body they belonged or to-day belong. They
have sincerely served the cause of the spirit. They
are to us constant sources of religious insight. Even
the cynics and the rebels, whom we cited in our
opening lecture, have been, in many individual
cases, devoutly religious souls who simply could not
see the light as they consciously needed to see it,
and who loyally refused to lie for convention's sake.
Such have often served the cause of the spirit with
a fervour that you ill understand so long as their
words merely shock you. They often seem as if
they were hostile to the unity of the spirit. But,
in many cases, it is the narrowness of our nature,
the chaos of our unspiritual passions, the barren
formalism of our conventions that they assail. And
such assaults turn our eyes upward to the unity of

the spirit from whence alone consolation and escape may come. Indirectly, therefore, such souls are often the misunderstood prophets of new ways of salvation for men. When they are loyal, when their very hardness is due to their resolute truthfulness, they are often amongst the most effective friends of a deeper religious life.

A notable criterion whereby, quite apart from mere conventions, you may try the spirits that pretend or appear to be religious, and may discern the members of the invisible church from those who are not members, is the criterion of the prophet Amos: "Woe unto them that are at ease in Zion." This, as I said earlier, is one of the favourite tests applied by moralists for distinguishing those who serve from those who merely enjoy. That it is also a religious test, and *why* it is a religious test, our acquaintance with the spirit of loyalty has shown us. Religion, when triumphant, includes, indeed, the experience of inward peace; but the peace which is not won through strenuous loyal service is deceitful and corrupting. It is the conquest over and through tribulation which saves. Whoever conceives religion merely as a comfortable release from sorrows, as an agreeable banishment of cares, as a simple escape from pain, knows not what evil is, or what our human nature is, or what our need of salvation means, or what the will of the master of life demands. Therefore, a visible church that appears simply in the form of a cure for worry, or a preventive of trouble, seems to me to be lacking in a full sense of what loyalty is. Worry is indeed, in itself, not a religious exercise. But it is often an effective preliminary, and is sometimes, according to the vicissitudes of natural temper, a relatively harmless accompaniment, to a deeply religious life. Certainly the mere absence of worry, the mere attainment of a sensuous tranquillity, is no criterion of membership in the invisible church. Better a cynic or a rebel against conventional religious forms, or a pessimist, or a worrying soul, if only such a being is strenuously loyal according to his lights, than one to whom religion means simply a tranquil adoration without loyalty. But, of course, many of the tranquil are also loyal. When this is true we can only rejoice in their attainments.

If we look for other examples still of types of spirituality which seem to imply membership in the invisible church, I myself know of few better instances of the genuinely religious spirit than those which are presented to us, in recent times, by the more devoted servants of the cause of any one of the advancing natural sciences. And such instances are peculiarly instructive, because many great men of science, as a result of their personal temperament and training, are little interested in the forms of the visible church, and very frequently are loath to admit that their calling has religious bearings. But when the matter is rightly viewed, one sees that the great scientific investigator is not only profoundly loyal, but serves a cause which, at the present time, probably does more to unify every sort of wholesome human activity, to bind in one all the higher interests of humanity, to bring men of various lands and races close together in spirit than does any other one special cause that modern men serve. The cause of any serious scientific investigator is, from my point of view, a superhuman cause, for precisely the reasons which I have already explained to you.

The individual scientific worker, uninterested as he usually is in metaphysics, and unconcerned as he often is about the relation of his task to the interests of the visible church, knows indeed that with all his heart, and soul, and mind, and strength he serves a cause that he conceives to be worthy. He knows, also, that this cause is beneficent, and that it plays a great part in the directing of human activities, whether because his science already has practical applications, or because the knowledge of nature is in itself an elevating and enlarging influence for mankind. The scientific investigator knows also that, while his individual experience is the source to which he personally looks for new observations of facts, his private observations contribute to science only in so far as other investigators can verify his results. Hence his whole scientific life consists in submitting all his most prized discoveries to the rigid test of an estimate that belongs to no individual human experience, but that is, or that through loyal efforts tends to become, the common possession of the organised experience of all the workers in his field. So far the devoted investigator goes in his own consciousness as to his work.

Beyond this point, in estimating his ideals and his value, he sometimes seems not to wish to go, either because he is unreflective or because he is modest. But when we remember that the unity of human experience, in the light of which scientific results are tested, and to whose growth and enrichment the scientific worker is devoted, is indeed a superhuman reality of the type that we have now discussed; when we also recall the profound values which the scientific ideal has for all departments of human life in our day; when, further, we see how resolutely the true investigator gives his all to contribute to what is really the unity of the spirit, we may well wonder who is in essence more heartily religious than the completely devoted scientific investigator—such a man, for instance, as was Faraday.

When I have the fortune to hear of really great scientific workers who are as ready to die for their science (if an experiment or an observation requires risk) as to live for it through years of worldly privation and of rigid surrender of private interests to truth, and when I then by chance also hear that some of them were called, or perhaps even called themselves, irreligious men, I confess that I think of the little girl who walked by Wordsworth's side on the beach at Calais. The poet estimated her

variety of religious experience in words that I feel
moved to apply to the ardently loyal hero of science:

> "Thou dwellest in Abraham's bosom all the year,
> And worship'st at the temple's inmost shrine,
> God being with thee when we know it not."

There also exists a somewhat threadbare verse of
the poet Young which tells us how "the undevout
astronomer is mad." I should prefer to say that the
really loyal scientific man who imagines himself undevout is not indeed mad at all, but, like Wordsworth's young companion at Calais, unobservant of
himself and of the wondrous and beautiful love that
inspires him. For he is, indeed, inspired by a love
for something much more divine than is that august assemblage of mechanical and physical phe-
nomena called the starry heavens. The soul of his
work is the service of the unity of the spirit in one
of its most exalted forms.

That all who, belonging to any body of the visible
church, are seriously loyal to the divine according
to their lights, are members also of the invisible
church, needs, after what I have said, no further
explanation.

But if, surveying this multitude that no man can
number from every kindred, and tribe, and nation,
and tongue, you say that entrance to the invisible
church is guarded by barriers that seem to you not
high enough or strong enough, I reply that this
membership is indeed tested by the severest of rules.

Do you serve with all your heart, and soul, and mind, and strength a cause that is superhuman and that is indeed divine? This is the question which all have to answer who are to enter this the most spiritual of all human brotherhoods.

IV

The invisible church is to be to us a source of insight. This means that we must enter into some sort of communion with the faithful if we are to enjoy the fruits of their insight. And, apart from one's own life of loyal service itself, the principal means of grace—that is, the principal means of attaining instruction in the spirit of loyalty, encouragement in its toils, solace in its sorrows, and power to endure and to triumph—the principal means of grace, I say, which is open to any man lies in such communion with the faithful and with the unity of the spirit which they express in their lives. It is natural that we should begin this process of communion through direct personal relations with the fellow-servants of our own special cause. Hence whatever is usually said by those who belong to any section of the visible church regarding the spiritual advantages which follow from entering the communion of their own body may be accepted, from our present point of view, as having whatever truth the devotion and the religious life of any one body of faithful servants of the unity of the spirit may give to such statements when applied precisely to their own members. But to us all alike the voice of the invisible church speaks—it sustains us all alike by its counsels, not merely in so far as our own personal cause and our brethren of that service are known to us, but in so far as we are ready to understand the loyal life, and to be inspired by it, even when those who exemplify its intents and its values are far from us in their type of experience and in the manner of their service.

You remember the rule of loyalty: "So serve your cause that if possible through your service everybody whom you influence shall be rendered a more devoted servant of his own cause, and thereby of the cause of causes—the unity of all the loyal." Now the rule for using the invisible church as a source of insight is this: "So be prepared to interpret, and sympathetically to comprehend, the causes and the service of other men, that whoever serves the cause of causes, the unity of all the loyal, may even thereby tend to help you in your personal service of your own special cause." To cultivate the comprehension and the reverence for loyalty, however, and wherever loyalty may be found, is to prepare yourself for a fitting communion with the invisible church.

And in such communion I find the crowning source of religious insight. What I say is wholly consistent then with the recognition of the preciousness of the visible church to its members. Once more, however, I point out the fact that the visible church is as precious as it is because it is indeed devoted to the unity of the spirit, that is, because it is a part and an organ of the invisible church.

V

I cannot close this extremely imperfect sketch of our crowning source of insight without applying to our present doctrine of the invisible church, the eternally true teaching of St. Paul regarding spiritual gifts.

As Paul's Corinthians, in their little community, faced the problem of the diversity of the gifts and powers whereby their various members undertook to serve the common cause—as this diversity of gifts tended from the outset to doctrinal differences of opinion, as the differences threatened to confuse loyalty by bringing brethren into conflict—even so, but with immeasurably vaster complications, the whole religious world, the invisible community of the loyal, has always faced, and still faces, a diversity of powers and of forms of insight, a diversity due to the endlessly various temperaments, capacities and sorts and conditions of men. The Corinthian church, as Paul sketched its situation, was a miniature of religious humanity. All the ways that the loyal follow lead upward to the realm of the spirit, where reason is at once the overarching heaven and the all-vitalising devotion which binds

every loyal individual to the master of life. But
in our universe the one demands the many. The
infinite becomes incarnate through the finite. The
paths that lead the loyal to the knowledge of the
eternal pass for our vision, with manifold crossings
and with perplexing wanderings, through the wilderness of this present world. The divine life is won
through suffering. And religious history is a tale
of suffering—of mutual misunderstanding amongst
brethren who have from moment to moment been
able to remember God only by narrowly misreading
the hearts of their brethren. The diversity of spiritual gifts has developed, in religious history, an
endless war of factions. The invisible church has
frequently come to consciousness in the form of
sects that say: "Ours alone is the true spiritual gift.
Through our triumph alone is the world to be saved.
Man will reach salvation only when our own Jerusa-
lem is the universally recognised holy city."

Now it is useless to reduce the many to the one
merely by wiping out the many. It is useless to
make some new sect whose creed shall be that there
are to be no sects. *The unity of the visible church,
under any one creed, or with any one settled system
of religious practices, is an unattainable and undesir-
able ideal.* The varieties of religious experience in
James's sense of that term are endless. The diversity of gifts is as great as is the diversity of
strong and loyal personalities. What St. Paul saw,
in the miniature case presented to him by the Co-

rinthian church, was that all the real gifts, and all
the consequently inevitable differences of approach
to the religious problems, and all the differences of
individual religious insight were necessary to a
wealthy religious life, and might serve the unity
of the spirit, if only they were conceived and used
subject to the spiritual gift which he defined as
Charity.

Now the Pauline Charity is simply *that* form of
loyalty which should characterise a company of
brethren who already have recognised their brotherhood, who consciously know that their cause is
one and that the spirit which they serve is one.   For
such brethren, loyalty naturally takes the form of a
self-surrender that need not seek its own, or assert
itself vehemently, because the visible unity of the
community in question is already acknowledged by
all the faithful present, so that each intends to edify,
not himself alone, but his brethren, and also intends
not to convert his brother to a new faith, but to es-
tablish him in a faith already recognised by the community.   Yet since the Corinthians, warring over
their diversity of gifts, had come to lose sight of the
common spirit, Paul simply recalls them to their
flag, by his poem of charity, which is also a technically true statement of how the principle of loyalty
applies to a brotherhood fully conscious of its common aim.

But the very intimacy of the Pauline picture of
charity makes it hard to apply this account of the

loyalty that should reign within a religious family
to the problems of a world where faith does not
understand faith, where the contrasts of opinion
seem to the men in question to exclude community
of the spirit, where the fighting blood even of saintly
souls is stirred by persecutions or heated by a hatred of seemingly false creeds. And Paul himself
could not speak in the language of charity, either
when he referred to those whom he called "false
brethren" or characterised the Hellenic-Roman spiritual world to whose thought and spirit he owed
so much. As the Corinthians, warring over the
spiritual gifts, were a miniature representation of
the motives that have led to religious wars, so St.
Paul's own failure to speak with charity as soon as
certain matters of controversy arose in his mind,
shows in miniature the difficulty that the visible
church, in all its forms, has had to unite loyal strenuousness of devotion to the truth that one sees with
tolerance for the faiths whose meaning one cannot
understand.

And yet, what Paul said about charity must be
universalised if it is true. When we universalise
the Pauline Charity, it becomes once more the loyalty that, as a fact, is now justified in seeking her
loyal own; but that still, like charity, rejoices in
the truth. Such loyalty loves loyalty even when
race or creed distinctions make it hard or impossible
for us to feel fond of the persons and practices
and opinions whereby our more distant brethren

embody their spiritual gifts. Such loyalty is tolerant. Tolerance is what charity becomes when we have to deal with those whose special cause we just now cannot understand. Loyalty is tolerant, *not* as if truth were indifferent, or as if there were no contrast between worldliness and spirituality, but is tolerant precisely in so far as the best service of loyalty and of religion and of the unity of the spirit consists in helping our brethren not to our own, but to *their* own. *Such loyalty implies genuine faith in the abiding and supreme unity of the spirit.*

Only by thus universalising the doctrine which Paul preached to the Corinthians can we be prepared to use to the full this crowning source of insight—the doctrine, the example, the life, the inspiration, which is embodied in the countless forms and expressions of the invisible church.

The work of the invisible church—it is just that work to which all these lectures have been directing your attention. The sources of insight are themselves the working of its spirit in our spirits.

If I have done anything (however unworthy) to open the minds of any of you to these workings, my fragmentary efforts will not have been in vain. I have no authority to determine your own insight. Seek insight where it is to be found.

INDEX

By Frank M. Oppenheim, S.J.

299